Energizers!

88 Quick Movement Activities That Refresh and Refocus

K-6

by Susan Lattanzi Roser

CENTER FOR RESPONSIVE SCHOOLS, INC.

All net proceeds from the sale of this book support the work of Center for Responsive Schools, Inc., a not-for-profit educational organization and the developer of the *Responsive Classroom*® approach to teaching.

ISBN: 978-1-892989-33-8
Library of Congress Control Number: 2009927687

Cover and book design by Helen Merena
Cover photograph by Jeff Woodward

Thanks to the children whose illustrations grace these pages.

Center for Responsive Schools, Inc.
85 Avenue A, P.O. Box 718
Turners Falls, MA 01376-0718

800-360-6332
www.responsiveclassroom.org

Eleventh printing 2019

DEDICATION

For Dad and Mom,

who instilled in me the love

of music and creativity,

and for my husband Mark

and my two boys, Will and Wes,

who keep the playful and energetic

girl in me alive today.

ACKNOWLEDGMENTS

So many people have guided me, supported me, and been models for me during the time I wrote this book, as well as throughout my life:

My sister Laura, my first example of "an adult" who found joy in being playful and creative with me and other children. I still today play with my own children and students in a way she played with me.

My niece Elizabeth Sterling, without whom we would not have such beautiful musical notation for the energizers. I appreciate your patience and expertise in translating the tunes to accurate notation.

Colleen and Fred Bretthauer, my dear musical friends whose talent in making music meaningful for children is one I will always honor and appreciate. Thank you for playfully enduring many gatherings where we practiced the energizers together.

Priscilla Donham, my first mentor teacher, who modeled playfulness in a way that built strong relationships with our preschoolers on a daily basis. She believed in me and helped me soar to new heights.

Hugh Hanley, a music teacher who visited our preschool classroom and taught me about the power of chanting, singing, and being creative with children.

Jean Cagianello and Allison Haines, for the team-teaching years of laughter, support, and encouragement around bringing the arts and creativity into our classrooms.

Marlynn Clayton, who first brought to life for me the value and purpose of playfulness in the classroom.

Mary Beth Forton, Elizabeth Nash, and Alice Yang, who as my editors guided and supported me through this process and so carefully and expertly organized my words into a well-orchestrated manuscript.

Helen Merena, whose graphic design talent made this book beautiful and enjoyable to read and learn from.

My dear friends and colleagues Carol Davis, Caltha Crowe, Leslie Alexander, Melissa Correa-Connolly, Andy Dousis, Tina Valentine, Marcia Bradley, Babs Freeman-Loftis, Eileen Mariani, Paula Denton, Courtney Fox, and Lynn Majewski, all of whom directly or indirectly gave their time to me on e-mail, on the phone, or in person as I processed so many pieces of the book. Thank you for helping me believe that my voice is worth sharing with other teachers.

My family—you too, Joanie—for playing and experimenting with me over and over again as I worked on the energizers in this book. Thanks also for understanding when I couldn't be with you because I had to write just a little bit more.

And lastly, but most importantly, my dear husband Mark, who is always there for me in a way that words cannot describe. Thank you for all the guidance, patience, and encouragement through this journey of struggles and celebrations.

CONTENTS

Energize! i

Finding the Right Energizer xi

88 Energizers xv

29. Hand Dance

30. Have a Ball

31. Head, Shoulders, Knees & Toes

32. High Low Up & Down

33. Hot Tamale

34. Human Protractor

35. I Feel the Same Way

36. Imagine This

37. Interruptions

38. Laughing Handkerchief

39. Left and Right

40. Let's Get the Rhythm

41. Lyle Crocodile

42. Ma Zinga!

43. Mirrors

44. Mosquito

45. Mumbo Jumbo Bubblegum

46. My Bonny

47. My Favorite Sport

48. My Sweet Old Aunt

49. My Two Hands

50. Never-Ending Word

51. No-Talk Toss

52. Now I'm Still

53. Number Freeze

54. Oh, My!

55. Oliver Twist

56. Opposite World Freeze Dance

57. Pass the Mask

58. People to People

59. Popcorn's in the Popper

60. Pop-Up Number

61. Rainstorm

62. Ram Sam Sam

63. Robot Rap

64. Row Your Boat

65. Save the Earth

66. Set the Table

67. Shake It

68. Shake It Down

69. Shante Ohm

70. Share the Light

71. Shark Attack

72. Solar System Rap

73. Song of the Day

74. Spelling Stroll

75. Sports on the Move

76. Switch!

77. Tarzan

78. Terry the Towel

79. Tony Chestnut

80. Top It

81. Walkie-Talkies

82. The Wave

83. We're All Back Together Again

84. What's the Connection?

85. Which Direction?

86. World Ocean Doo-Wop

87. Worldwide Seven Continents

88. Za Ziggy

Energize!

Teachers know it instinctively, they see it every day in their classrooms, and research supports it: To feel well and learn well, children need to move. And they need to move at regular intervals throughout their school day, not just at recess or during after-school free play. Children's movement expert Jean Blaydes Madigan offers these thoughts on how movement helps learning:

> *Daily exercise cements the details learned in the previous 48 hours. If*
> *that physical activity doesn't take place, anywhere from 20% to 80%*
> *of that learned cognitive information is lost. . . . When you sit longer*
> *than 17 minutes . . . your brain essentially tells your body, "You can*
> *go to sleep because no movement has occurred."* (Madigan, n.d.)

Yet even though we know how important movement is for children, our packed school schedules often leave us feeling that we can't spare any time away from lessons. That's where the energizers in this book come in. In just two or three playful minutes, these energizers get children moving, breathing deeply, laughing, and singing or chanting together. Then, with spirits refreshed, bodies relaxed, and minds clear, they're ready to refocus on more—and more productive—learning.

Energizers are a playful, purposeful way to incorporate physical exercise and mental stimulation into an already tight day. Using energizers doesn't take much time, but it can make a big impact on learning.

SO WHAT IS AN ENERGIZER?

Energizers are quick whole-group activities that can be done anywhere and anytime in the school day. They can be lively or calming. They can have an academic component or can be just for fun. They can be used to transition children between learning activities, as a pick-me-up during intensive lessons, as a way to keep order during times of waiting, as a focusing tool to use when students are outside the classroom, and in many other ways. Energizers can be done with students in a circle, at their desks or tables, or even while they're waiting in a line. What a gift—joyful, purposeful, engaging activities to help ease students through the school day!

Energizers can be used for many reasons, but their primary purposes are to provide:

- *Mental and physical breaks:* The mind and body breaks that energizers provide help students refocus their energy and be better prepared for learning.

- *Connections through play:* Energizers provide a quick, safe, and structured way for teachers to connect with their students.

- *Focusing:* Energizers help gain students' attention when they may otherwise be distracted.

Mental and physical breaks

Energizers give learners' minds and bodies both a physical and mental break from the previous lesson or focus of study. When we move, our bodies feed our brains oxygen, water, and glucose—substances essential to the brain's ability to learn. Movement also stimulates brain cells to bind together in a way that supports learning (Pica, 2006; Ratey, 2008). Researchers have found that a break in concentration every twenty minutes increases students' productivity, the quality of their work, and their morale—and the younger the student, the more dramatic the results (Erlauer, 2003).

Breaks can occur in many ways, and you're probably already using many of them. For example, you may give an example or tell a brief story to illustrate a point. Perhaps you build in interactive teaching structures such as partner or small group work, give learners time to reflect, incorporate humor that often leads to laughter . . . you get the idea. The specialty of the energizers in this book is that they give you many more structures that not only help the brain shift gears, but also help the whole physical body release any stored-up energy in a playful, purposeful, community-building way.

Both types of energizers—the quite active ones and those that are more calming—meet the need for the brain to shift, change, or stop what it's doing, refresh itself, and feel alive for the next task at hand. Once the energizer is over, your learners will be ready to listen and take on the next task much more successfully.

Connections through play

We need to find ways to develop deeper relationships with our students, for as studies show, those students who have positive connections with their teachers experience the most success in school and in life. In addition to addressing the brain's need for physical breaks and exercise, play between teachers and students creates a bond that allows both to experience each other in a natural, friendly way. It's an opportunity for students to see another side of their teacher.

As play continues swiftly disappearing from our schools to be replaced with more academics, it is critical that we as teachers find ways to incorporate play throughout the day. By demonstrating a willingness to play, the teacher models risk-taking, success, and failure. This in turn empowers the students to take their own risks with each other and in their academic learning. So take time to be playful with your students.

Focusing

When students are distracted, whether by their peers, outside interferences, or their own daydreams, energizers are an excellent tool to help them get back to the task at hand. Or perhaps they're in line, waiting for the specials teacher to show up (who's late because she's doing an awesome energizer with her previous group!) and just can't stay quiet. Incorporate an energizer. Try a lively one like "Robot Rap" (number 63) or a follow-the-leader game like "The Doctor Says" (number 19). These quick, whole-group activities give you positive ways to playfully get your students' attention and focus their energy as a group.

SINGING IN THE MUSIC ROOM VERSUS THE CLASSROOM

Now, if you're a music teacher, you may be thinking, "Well, what about music literacy? I need to develop my students' 'ears' for music! I need to teach them to read and write notation! I need to get them to keep a steady beat!"

As a pianist myself, I completely recognize the importance of proper teaching when it comes to musical notation, tonal patterns, rhythm accuracy, time signatures, pitch, performance, etc. But energizers are not about replacing music instruction. They are about developing a love for music and playfulness in the standard self-contained classroom. They're about the power of community learning through multiple joyful experiences, one of them being sing-alongs. We all appreciate and treasure the sounds of sing-alongs going on in the classrooms as we walk down the hallways. And we classroom teachers know that the necessities for teaching music literacy will be handled with confidence and skill by our fellow music-teaching experts.

HOW TO USE ENERGIZERS: TWELVE TIPS

1. Know your students—and yourself

Let your knowledge of your students guide your choice of energizers. For each energizer, I give suggested grade levels, but you're the best judge of whether an energizer fits the developmental level of your particular class. You're also the best judge of the children's energy levels—how they cycle through the day, as a group and as individuals, and what the class mood is at any particular moment.

It's also important that you feel comfortable doing the energizers you choose. Perhaps you may feel embarrassed about dancing or using a silly voice. Honor that! We know that children are always watching their teachers. If you're feeling reluctant or shy, the children may respond in the same way.

Do keep in mind, though, that by embracing our discomfort with an energizer and doing it anyway, we provide our children with the courage to do the same. With the right environment, a caring community where we can feel safe to mess up and still be accepted, a place where all ideas are honored, we can learn to discover the creative artist inside ourselves. Let your artist come out. If there is any audience who will welcome it with open and loving hearts, it's the children you teach. And what a powerful model you will be for them to take a risk—just as you did.

There are plenty of energizers to choose from, so use ones that both you and your students are comfortable with and adapt them to suit your style. As you and the class become more comfortable and experienced in using energizers, you might decide to try some that originally felt risky.

2. Model how to do each energizer

Even though you can do all of these energizers in just three minutes or less, you'll need to do some initial teaching with your students before you use an energizer. Interactive Modeling (in which children watch you demonstrate a behavior and comment on what they see you doing) is a good way to teach children anything involving actions. Here's how Interactive Modeling might look if you were teaching the "Double This Double That" energizer (number 20).

Interactive Modeling Steps	Possible Teacher Language	Possible Student Responses
Say what you will model and why.	*When doing this chant with a partner, we need to follow our rule of being safe. We'll all need to be friendly and gentle.*	
Model the behavior.	*Watch Wesley and me as we do the chant together in a safe and friendly way.*	
Ask students what they noticed.	*What did you notice about what we did? How was it safe? In what ways were we friendly?*	*You looked at him.* *Your face was smiling.* *You patted hands softly.*
Invite one or more students to model.	*Who else would like to show us a friendly and careful way to do the chant with a partner? . . . OK, let's all watch carefully as Will and AJ do the chant together.*	
Again, ask students what they noticed.	*What did you see Will and AJ do?*	*They patted hands gently, like you and Wesley.* *They had happy voices, but not too loud.* *They smiled at each other.*
Have all students practice.	*Looks like you're all ready to try the chant with a partner. I'll watch you all do it just the way we saw it demonstrated. Let's go!*	
Provide feedback.	*We were safe, friendly, and lively during our chant. We really worked well together!*	

3. Take your time

Especially for those energizers that are a bit more complex (such as "Carousel," number 11), keep in mind that it's fine to scaffold the energizers—to introduce and practice the energizer components slowly, over several teaching periods, if necessary. After all, the goal of using energizers is to relax and have fun! So give yourself and the children plenty of time to feel comfortable with an energizer's words and actions before doing it "for real."

Also keep in mind that tempo is important. Doing an energizer faster doesn't always mean having more fun. Speeding up too soon can frustrate children. Speed can bring on laughter and foster engagement, but only after your students have shown success in doing the energizer. The same goes for adding other variables, such as louder voices or more movements.

4. Make each energizer your own

Energizers are like folk songs and storytelling combined. We hear them once, try them out for ourselves, learn them well through trial and error, and then share them with others. As energizers pass on from person to person and year to year, elements change a bit as each person does them his or her own way. Knowing that energizers reflect the joyful thoughts of many people makes them even more fun.

So try out the energizers in this book the way I explain them, and then make them your own. Feel free to improvise. Don't know the tune? Make up your own. Can't catch the exact rhythm? Ask your students to come up with one that goes with the words. Forgot the words? Hum or sing *la-la-la*. Your creative, on-the-spot substitutions will invigorate the children and help them trust their own creativity and sense of fun.

You can also have fun varying an energizer's words, rhythm, pace, or volume. Add some new verses using the children's ideas. Try a different rhythm for a chant or a different tune for a song. Sing the words in slow motion with exaggerated voice tones and body movements. Notch up the speed and the volume. Or try speeding up while being quiet—trickier than you might think!

Before long, you may find yourself making up your own energizers. That's how it happened for me. As I used energizers others had taught me, I found myself making up my own to suit various situations in my classroom. You'll see my creations marked with "Original by the author." I hope they'll encourage you to create your own energizers!

5. Invite the children's ideas

Once the children feel comfortable with an energizer, ask for their ideas on different tunes, tones, and actions. They'll have more fun if they have a role in making the energizer unique to their class.

Using the children's ideas has several side benefits, too. Knowing that their ideas matter develops children's self-confidence and encourages them to continue thinking for themselves. And knowing that they can learn from each other as well as from you builds community.

Strong leaders know when to invite their audience for their thoughts and hold back on sharing their own ideas. They also know when it's most effective and efficient to just tell their groups the best way to carry out an activity. Open-ended conversations sometimes have a tendency to go too long. Instead of helping children focus and participate, such conversations may inadvertently create the opposite effect: unfocused listeners who become frustrated in having to listen to someone else's far-out idea.

6. Repeat the children's favorites

You may be wondering if you have to continually try different energizers with your class. Will the children get bored with an energizer if you repeat it? The good news is that most children enjoy repeating a fun, developmentally appropriate energizer with reasonable frequency, say two or three times a week. The familiarity lends a sense of security and competence, and the children enjoy sharing a classroom routine.

Another benefit of repeating energizers is that there's more to learn from the energizer each time children do it, especially if you focus each time on something slightly different. For example, if you've taught "Rainstorm" (number 61) as a whole-group energizer, you could divide the children into two or three groups and have three rainstorms, each starting a second or two after the other. Or you could vary "Ram Sam Sam" (number 62) by using six-inch voices for the words or even saying the words in your heads as you try to keep the beat.

So repetition is fine, but keep an eye on the children's interest level and try new energizers before they—or you—tire of their favorites.

7. Find ways to include reluctant students

Shy and reluctant children have the same needs for belonging, significance, and fun as all other children, yet they may feel uncomfortable doing energizers with the class. They may, however, be happy to take a more indirect role. Shy children can point to the words on the chart while the class sings. They can be eyewitnesses, watching the class carefully and then sharing three adjectives that describe what they saw the class doing. Or you can entrust shy children with the responsibility of turning the lights off when it's time for a quiet energizer and back on when it's over.

When you help children meet their needs in ways that feel comfortable to them, they'll very likely respond positively. And the next time or two you do the energizer, you may be pleasantly surprised to see them join in.

8. Write out songs and chants

We want our students to participate, to feel comfortable joining in. With energizers, sometimes the reason children don't chant or sing along is simply that they don't know the words!

Song charts like the sample shown on the next page will help students who are learning to read or still mastering the words of a particular song. The charts will also come in handy for a substitute teacher to use when you're out of the classroom. Your students will feel empowered to guide their "guest teacher" in doing some of their favorite energizers.

As on the sample chart, be sure to put each phrase of the song on a separate line, rather than running all the lines together paragraph style.

Deep and Wide

Deep and wide
Deep and wide
There's a river flowing
Deep and wi-ide!
Deep and wide
Deep and wide
There's a river flowing
Deep and wide!

9. Join in and SING!

Raising our voices in celebration is natural. Fans chant and cheer together at sports events; students spontaneously break into a chant while on the school bus for a field trip; friends gathered together burst into a song they all remember from high school or college. No matter how different we are in some ways, when we do such things together, we're building community around a shared repertoire of songs and chants.

When you do energizers with your students, you're building community in your classroom, no matter what your singing talents are. So don't worry about performing for your students. It's more important that you join in and sing or chant with your students. Children really don't care how we sound when we're all singing playfully together! What they notice and remember is not how well you sing with them, but that you do sing with them, in a way that's genuine and joyful.

Remember, too, that with all of these energizers (including those with musical notation), singing is just an option. Children will have just as much fun if you skip the tune and simply chant or say the words to any easy-to-follow beat you choose. Do whatever feels comfortable to you and your students!

10. Sing high

When you model an energizer for children, they'll learn most quickly and have the most fun if they can fairly accurately reproduce the sound of your voice. Children naturally sing about an octave or two higher than adults, so you'll want to use your highest voice when singing with them.

Remember that energizers are all about having fun, so it doesn't matter a bit if you have a shaky high voice or lack perfect pitch.

11. Plan how to end lively energizers

Certainly many energizers will liven up your students—that's one of their purposes. But it's also important to keep this liveliness within reasonable limits and to help children calm themselves as they finish an exuberant energizer so they can focus on their learning. Here are some tips:

- For energizers that end with slowing or sitting down, overemphasize the settling down movements when you model for the children. As the children practice, encourage them: "Wow! That was fun! I see you're all sitting down now, taking some deep breaths, becoming more quiet, and looking up at me. You're really ready for what's coming next."

- End with a rhyming chant that naturally directs the children to a seated position. "My Two Hands" (number 49) is magical for this.

- Hold up your five fingers while singing a downward scale as you fold down each finger one at a time: *5 . . . 4 . . . 3 . . . 2 . . . 1 . . . shhhh*. End with your index finger on your mouth as you say *shhhh* very softly.

- Use a quiet signal. When well taught, modeled, and practiced, quiet signals reliably get children's undivided attention. A raised hand, a gentle chime, a rain stick, a clapping pattern that the class echoes, or any auditory signal the children are familiar with will help them transition to the next task.

- If children are struggling to gain self-control, use calm but firm redirecting language to end the activity: "Stop. Everyone take a seat. We're being too wild and noisy, so we have to end right away. We'll try again tomorrow."

12. Remind yourself that it's okay to play!

Not only is it okay for teachers to play with children, it's important to the children's learning. Through shared play, we can model risk-taking, cooperation, self-control, and assertiveness, all skills important to children's success in school and in life.

Engaging with children in appropriate, structured play also lets us experience each other in an informal, friendly way. The "play bond" we form fosters positive relationships with our students, and research shows us that children who have positive connections with their teachers experience more success in school—and in life.

USING THIS BOOK

To quickly find energizers that fit the needs of your class, check the grids on pages xii–xiv. They categorize all 88 energizers by grade level and purpose. Remember, though, that the grade levels I've given are just guidelines. You can adapt most of the energizers in this book to work well with children of any age. For example, you could adapt the "Spelling Stroll" (number 74) to fit K–2 children by using sight words or their names. With the "Never-Ending Word" category game (number 50), younger children could call out the name of anything that fits in the designated category, rather than calling out words that start with the last letter of the previous word.

For energizers including sung or chanted words (and most of them do), italic type distinguishes the words of the energizer from instructions and comments. Where the beat is important, bold italic type shows you which words or parts of words to emphasize.

I've included simple musical notation for some energizers that use songs, but you needn't read music to use and enjoy those energizers. You can always chant the words instead of singing them, or use another tune you already know.

A FEW LAST THOUGHTS

Educator or entertainer? I believe we teachers need to be a little bit of both. As teachers, we are educators first. And yes, in all my years of teaching, and in all my years of consulting, I have seen teachers who are all too entertaining. But I've also seen some who are all too educational. It can be easy for some of us to find the educator in ourselves, and it can feel silly or irresponsible to use the entertainer in ourselves. Don't feel guilty about it. Know its purpose, know its place, know its limits. And go for it. Our kids, our classrooms—our world—can always use a little more playfulness and laughter. Relish it, release it, and spread it around. Laughter is contagious. And I believe it is the best medicine. Make it your and your students' daily supplement, in quick, small doses. You'll be pleasantly surprised how healthy you'll all feel—mentally, physically, and intellectually.

As you go into your classroom and look for ways to give your children a mental and physical break, try an energizer. When your students are distracted, refocus them with an old favorite. When you need to connect with your students, take a risk and be playful. Relax, experiment, trust your abilities, and ENERGIZE!

REFERENCES

Erlauer, L. (2003). *The Brain-Compatible Classroom: Using What We Know about Learning to Improve Teaching*. Alexandria, VA: ASCD.

Madigan, J.B. (n.d.). *"Why 30 Minutes of Exercise Is Important."* Retrieved May 4, 2009, from http://www.actionbasedlearning.com/articles.shtml.

Pica, R. (2006). *A Running Start: How Play, Physical Activity, & Free Time Create a Successful Child*. New York: Marlowe & Company.

Ratey, J. (2008). *Spark: The Revolutionary New Science of Exercise and the Brain*. New York: Little, Brown and Company.

Finding the Right Energizer

The energizers in the grids that follow are arranged alphabetically and by four categories:

- *Movers/Shakers* involve lively large motor movement.

- *Calmers/Relaxers* are quieter energizers and typically take place with students seated or standing calmly. They do not involve large movements.

- *Chants* are simply rhymes vocalized and clapped to a beat. They work wonderfully when transitioning children from one activity to another. Simply begin the chant when about a third of the class has joined you, for example, in the meeting area, and before you know it the rest of the class will be with you doing the chant and ready for the next lesson.

- *Songs* are energizing in and of themselves! The songs in this book include motions, too.

ENERGIZERS FOR ALL GRADES (K–6)

	Movers/ Shakers	Calmers/ Relaxers	Chants	Songs	Number
Aroostasha	✿				5
Boom Chicka Boom	✿				9
Clapping Patterns			✿		14
Dum Dum Dah Dah	✿			✿	22
Froggie			✿		25
Funga Alafia				✿	26
Hand Dance	✿				29
Hot Tamale	✿				33
Human Protractor		✿			34
Laughing Handkerchief	✿				38
Ma Zinga!	✿				42
Mosquito			✿		44
My Favorite Sport	✿				47
Opposite World Freeze Dance	✿				56
Pass the Mask		✿			57
Pop-Up Number	✿				60
Rainstorm	✿				61
Row Your Boat				✿	64
Shante Ohm			✿		69
Share the Light		✿			70
Solar System Rap			✿		72
Song of the Day				✿	73
Sports on the Move	✿				75
World Ocean Doo-Wop				✿	86

	Movers/ Shakers	Calmers/ Relaxers	Chants	Songs	Number
Alphabet Aerobics	❀				2
As Still As a Rock	❀				6
The Button Factory	❀				10
Clap Your Hands	❀				15
Deep and Wide	❀			❀	16
Dino Dinner Chant			❀		18
The Fidget Family	❀				23
Five Plump Peas			❀		24
Go Bananas	❀				27
Granny at the Fair	❀		❀		28
Head, Shoulders, Knees & Toes	❀			❀	31
High Low Up & Down				❀	32
Interruptions		❀			37
Let's Get the Rhythm			❀		40
Lyle Crocodile	❀				41
Mumbo Jumbo Bubblegum			❀		45
My Bonny	❀			❀	46
My Sweet Old Aunt	❀			❀	48
My Two Hands			❀		49
Now I'm Still	❀				52
Oh, My!			❀		54
Oliver Twist	❀				55
Popcorn's in the Popper	❀			❀	59
Ram Sam Sam	❀			❀	62
Robot Rap	❀			❀	63
Save the Earth	❀				65
Tarzan				❀	77
Terry the Towel	❀				78
Tony Chestnut	❀			❀	79
We're All Back Together Again				❀	83
Worldwide Seven Continents			❀		87

ENERGIZERS FOR GRADES 3-6

	Movers/ Shakers	Calmers/ Relaxers	Chants	Songs	Number
Air Writing	✿				1
And Don't You Forget It!		✿			3
Answer This		✿			4
Awake, Alert, Alive	✿			✿	7
Body Drumming	✿				8
Carousel	✿				11
Chase the Bunny	✿				12
Check My Beat	✿				13
Did You Know?		✿			17
The Doctor Says	✿				19
Double This Double That	✿				20
Do What I Said, Not What I Say	✿				21
Have a Ball	✿				30
I Feel the Same Way	✿				35
Imagine This		✿			36
Left and Right	✿				39
Mirrors		✿			43
Never-Ending Word			✿		50
No-Talk Toss	✿				51
Number Freeze	✿				53
People to People	✿				58
Set the Table			✿		66
Shake It	✿				67
Shake It Down	✿				68
Shark Attack	✿				71
Spelling Stroll	✿				74
Switch		✿			76
Top It		✿			80
Walkie-Talkies	✿				81
The Wave	✿				82
What's the Connection?		✿			84
Which Direction?	✿				85
Za Ziggy	✿				88

Energizers!

Air Writing

A traditional way of practicing letters—with a twist.

GRADE LEVEL

3–6

SKILLS PRACTICED

Self-control, spelling, coordination

MATERIALS NEEDED

None

ACTIONS

Call out familiar words, such as the weekly spelling list or words from the word wall, as the children write them in the air with the pointer finger of their dominant hand, using either printing or cursive.

VARIATIONS

- Partner students up. Partners take turns choosing a familiar word to air write. The observer tries to guess which word the partner is air writing.

- Have the children write with progressively more challenging body parts (nondominant hand, elbow, shoulder, knee, foot, nose, hip, ear, entire body).

- Sing the Alphabet Song as you air write the letters.

Alphabet Aerobics

This one is a good all-over-body-stretcher, while kinesthetically reinforcing lowercase letter formation.

GRADE LEVEL

K–3

SKILLS PRACTICED

Focusing, listening, self-control, comprehension

MATERIALS NEEDED

A visual of the alphabet

WORDS

Chant the alphabet slowly.

ACTIONS

As the leader chants each letter's name, children imagine each lowercase letter in their minds (or refer to the classroom alphabet chart) and form the letter with their bodies.

For letters that "stand tall" on the writing lines (for example, b, d, f, h), stand straight up and lift arms straight up over head.

For letters in the middle of the writing lines (for example, a, c, e, i) stand straight, bend knees slightly, and place arms out straight ahead.

For letters with "tails" that drop below the writing line (for example, g, j, p, q), squat down and put hands on floor.

VARIATIONS

- Alpha-aerobic your name.

- Alpha-aerobic your spelling list.

- Once the children are comfortable and confident, speed it up!

And Don't You Forget It!

A great energizer for getting to know each other's names.

GRADE LEVEL

3–6

SKILLS PRACTICED

Focusing, memory, language arts

MATERIALS NEEDED

None

WORDS AND ACTIONS

In the beginning of the year, when students are still getting to know one another's names, use this as your focus. As children become more comfortable with each other's names, challenge them to name two children before them, then four, and so on.

Decide on an order for who will go first, next, etc. Children may be standing at their desks or tables or in a circle.

First student looks to the person next to him and says, *My name is _____, and don't you forget it!*

Next child in order says, *His name is _____, my name is _____, and don't you forget it!*

Continue going around the room, with each child repeating the name of the child before him or her.

VARIATIONS

Later in the year, when students know their classmates' names, challenge the group to do this energizer with other chosen topics. For example:

- Things you saw at the science museum
  I saw a dinosaur skeleton, and don't you forget it!

- Things you like to do outside
  Outside, Mary likes to jump rope, Will likes to slide, I like to swing, and don't you forget it!

- Things to remember to do when we write
  Wes remembers to use punctuation, Mark remembers to use creative vocabulary, I remember to use complete sentences, and don't you forget it!

"When children act out the words of a poem, the plot of a story, or the lyrics of a song, they must ponder the meanings of the words. And because those words are important to them—and such activities are fun—the poems, stories, and songs take on greater relevance. The children are also using multiple senses, which means more is learned and retained."

—Rae Pica, children's physical activity specialist

Answer This

The sillier the responses, the more fun the game! You can play this in a circle or line or with children at their desks or tables.

GRADE LEVEL

3–6

SKILLS PRACTICED

Listening, self-control, language arts

MATERIALS NEEDED

None

PREPARING STUDENTS FOR SUCCESS

If the children are at desks or tables, decide how each child will know when to take his or her turn.

WORDS

Pose a question to the class. Each student then provides one word that combines with the previous words to create a complete sentence and answer the question. For example:

Teacher: *How did the zebra get its stripes?*

Student	Word
1	*Long*
2	*long*
3	*ago*
4	*there*
5	*was*
6	*a*
7	*horse*
8	*that*
9	*ate*
10	*black*
11	*and*
12	*white*
13	*beans.*

In this example, the next round would start with the 14th student. Continue in this pattern until all have had at least one chance to add a word.

VARIATION

To add more energy, invite students to stand up as they say their word.

5

Aroostasha

A silly add-on movement chant.

PRONUNCIATION

ă-**roos**-tă-shă

GRADE LEVEL

K–6

SKILLS PRACTICED

Focusing, listening, self-control, empathy

MATERIALS NEEDED

None

PREPARING STUDENTS FOR SUCCESS

- Most often first taught in a circle, but once students know it, you can try it anywhere.

- Make sure students have space to bend forward and to move their arms safely from left to right. Discuss and practice how to do this safely while still being creative and having fun.

WORDS

Refrain for everyone (including leader):

Aroostasha!
Aroostasha!
Aroostasha-sha!

Aroostasha!
Aroostasha!
Aroostasha-sha!

Verse 1:

Leader: *Thumbs up!*
Group echoes: *Thumbs up!*
Everyone: Repeat "Aroostasha" refrain

Leader: *Thumbs up!*
Group echoes: *Thumbs up!*
Leader: *Wrists together!*
Group echoes: *Wrists together!*
Everyone: Repeat "Aroostasha" refrain

Verse 2:

Leader: *Thumbs up!*
Group echoes: *Thumbs up!*
Leader: *Wrists together!*
Group echoes: *Wrists together!*
Leader: *Elbows in!*
Group echoes: *Elbows in!*
Everyone: Repeat "Aroostasha" refrain

Continue the chant in this way, with the leader adding one more movement each time.

Possible additions:

Knees together!
Toes together!
Bottoms up!

ACTIONS

For the "Aroostasha" refrain, clasp your hands in front of you, interlacing your fingers. Move your clasped hands from the right side of your body to the left, pulsing your hands up and down to the beat.

As the leader calls out each movement, members add the movement to those they're already doing. For example, once you have your thumbs up, you keep them up and then hold your wrists together while keeping your thumbs up. Then, when the leader calls out elbows in, you keep your thumbs up and your wrists together while pulling your elbows in.

VARIATIONS

- Divide the class into two groups. One group can be the Aroostasha leaders and decide as a group beforehand what actions they will demonstrate. Be sure to first brainstorm appropriate motions that the group can do safely yet creatively.

- Invite two or three children to be co-leaders.

As Still As a Rock

An innovative version of the traditional "Freeze" game.

GRADE LEVEL

K–3

SKILLS PRACTICED

Listening, self-control, coordination

MATERIALS NEEDED

None

PREPARING STUDENTS FOR SUCCESS

- Discuss the rules for this game, sharing strategies on how to remain still. Share ideas about what positions this might be easiest with and which may pose a bigger challenge.

- Discuss what's okay to do (breathe!) and what's not okay to do (scratch your head, move your position, etc.).

- For "watchers," decide on a friendly way to let the leader know that a "rock" has moved.

ACTIONS

Tell the children to begin wandering around the room. After a half minute or so, call out, *Be still as a rock!* Everyone freezes. Wait until 30 seconds have elapsed. (You may want to begin with 5 or 10 seconds and work up to 30.) Then say, *Relax!*

Children continue wandering around the room until the next *Be still as a rock* command.

Children who talk, giggle, or move while being "rocks" become "watchers." They can help you "catch" any movers.

The challenge for the whole class is to see how many people can be still as rocks for the full 30 seconds. The children can share tips on ways to stay still.

Repeat several times, perhaps inviting different children to be the caller.

VARIATIONS

- Invite children to take turns as the "Be still as a rock!" caller.

- Choose different ways to move around the room—hopping, swaying, wiggling, bending over, stretching tall, dancing, etc. Model and practice safe ways to make the movements before doing them "for real."

Awake, Alert, Alive

A fun, challenging, energizer that fosters right brain-left brain agility as the hands cross the body's midline.

GRADE LEVEL

3–6

SKILLS PRACTICED

Memorization, rhythm, self-control, empathy

MATERIALS NEEDED

Optional: Chart with words

PREPARING STUDENTS FOR SUCCESS

- Practice singing the song together (can be sung to the tune "If You're Happy and You Know It").

- Model and practice actions for each word.

- Start slowly before speeding up!

- Share ways to support success within the group.

WORDS

I'm awake, alert, alive
Enthusiastic!
I'm awake, alert, alive
Enthusiastic!
I'm awake, alert, alive
Alive, alert, awake
Awake, alert, alive
Enthusiastic!

ACTIONS

Awake: Point to eyes

Alert: Point to brain

Alive: Cross arms over chest

Enthusiastic: Clap thighs once, clap hands once, snap fingers twice

VARIATIONS

- Once the class learns the words, challenge them by going faster and faster

- Try it in silence

Body Drumming

Make your bodies into a drum orchestra!

GRADE LEVEL

3–6

SKILLS PRACTICED

Self-control, focusing, rhythm

MATERIALS NEEDED

None

PREPARING STUDENTS FOR SUCCESS

Model with two students or with small groups before turning things over to the whole class.

ACTIONS

Begin by teaching the group a simple three-count stomp and clap pattern, such as:

Stomp ... stomp ... clap ...
stomp ... stomp ... clap ... etc.

Then teach the group a four-count pattern:

Stomp ... stomp ... stomp ... clap
Stomp ... stomp ... stomp ... clap ... etc.

Now divide the group in half and combine the stomps, one group doing the three-count pattern, the other doing the four count-pattern. It makes a really neat sound!

VARIATIONS

Create more elaborate patterns with various body drummings. For example, Group 1 does this pattern:

Clap ... clap ...
(cross arms) Shoulder tap ... shoulder tap ...
Thigh slap ... thigh slap ...
Stomp ... stomp ...

while group 2 does this pattern:

Clap
(cross arms) Shoulder tap ... shoulder tap ...
Thigh slap ... thigh slap ...
Stomp ... stomp ...

The first group is one step behind the second, creating a fascinating sound.

Boom Chicka Boom

A call and response movement chant. Have fun hamming it up!

GRADE LEVEL

K–6

SKILLS PRACTICED

Focusing, listening, self-control, creativity

MATERIALS NEEDED

None

WORDS

The leader says each line, and the group then repeats it, using the same intonation as the leader. Repeat the chant several times using a different volume or intonation each time.

Possible voices: Boisterous, falsetto, growly, whisper, baby

A boom chicka boom!
I said a boom chicka boom!
I said a booma chicka rocka, chicka rocka, chicka boom!
Oh yeah! [or *Okay!*]
Uh huh! [or *All right!*]
One more time!

VARIATIONS

Preface each verse by calling out what style it will be and adding motions as appropriate. For example:

Custodian style: Use the words "Broom Chicka Broom" and pretend to sweep

Rock-n-roll style: Pretend to play a guitar

Sleepy style: Use slow, sleepy voices

Robot style: Use clipped, monotone voices

Underwater style: Flap lips with fingers while singing

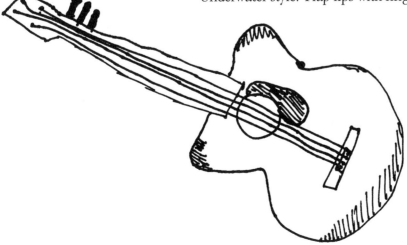

10 The Button Factory

An add-on movement game—you keep doing previous movements as you add new ones. It's a way to playfully challenge children's balance and coordination.

GRADE LEVEL

K–3

SKILLS PRACTICED

Focusing, listening, self-control, coordination

MATERIALS NEEDED

None

WORDS AND ACTIONS

Stand and recite the chant together, each time "pressing the button" with the additional body part while continuing to keep the previously named body part or parts in motion. You can replace the underlined words with other people or pets that might be in Joe's family.

Hi!
My name is Joe!
And I work in a button factory.
I have a wife and a dog and a family.
One day
The boss came along, he said,
"Joe … are you busy?"
I said, "No!"
"Then press the button with your right hand!"

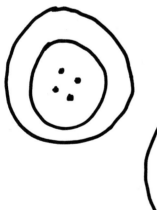
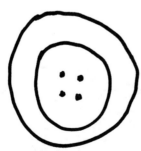
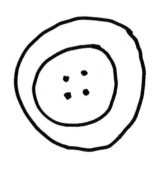

Repeat verse while pantomiming pressing button with right hand.

Repeat verse again, with the boss telling Joe to press the button with, for example, his left knee.

Repeat verse again while pantomiming pressing button with right hand and left knee.

Continue this pattern for several rounds.

To end

The boss came along, he said
"Joe … Are you busy?"
*I said, "**Yes**!!!"*

Carousel

A surprising noise-making activity that really does sound like a carousel. Done in a circle, it looks like one, too!

GRADE LEVEL

3–6

SKILLS PRACTICED

Focusing, listening, self-control

MATERIALS NEEDED

None

PREPARING STUDENTS FOR SUCCESS

Take your time teaching this one, especially if you want to do it in a moving circle.

- First, have the whole class do the sounds in unison, practicing correct enunciation and keeping a steady beat.

- Next, divide the class in half and have them practice doing just two of the sounds together. Work up to three and then four sounds.

- Then practice all four sounds with the children divided into four groups and standing in a line facing you. You'll be the carousel conductor, cuing each group when it's time to make their sound.

- Last, practice safely moving in a circle, first just walking and then walking with half the group standing up and half crouching down.

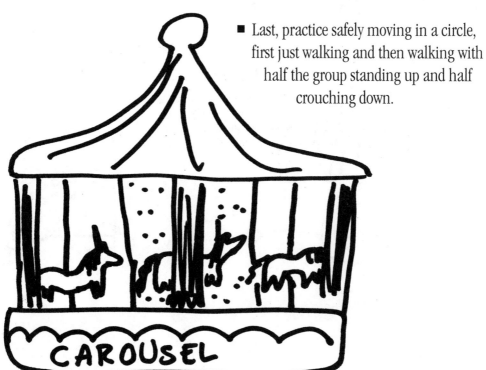

CAROUSEL

WORDS AND ACTIONS

Split the class into four separate groups and assign each a noise to make. The children can be in a straight line or a circle or even at their desks. Start with two groups standing and two crouching. With each repeat, each group changes position on the emphasized sounds—the standers crouch and the crouchers stand.

To get the carousel started, point to each group or call out "Group 1!" when it's time for them to make their sounds. Group 1 goes first with their sounds. After they've repeated their words two or three times, Group 2 chimes in with their sounds, while Group 1 continues with theirs, and so on, until all groups are saying their sounds at the same time.

Group 1: **Oom**-pa-pa

Group 2: **Oom**-sss-sss

Group 3: **Oom**-teedle-dee

Group 4: Na-na-**na**-na-na-na-**na**-na-na-**na**-na na **na** na. Na-na-**na**-na-na-na-**na**-na-na-**na**-na na **na!** (sung to the tune of "Did You Ever See a Lassie?")

ENDING

Starting with group 4, the groups go silent, one at a time, as you point to them, until only Group 1 is still going. After a few final *Oom-pa-pas*, you hold up your hand for "stop" (or use some other agreed-upon signal), and they become silent.

Chase the Bunny

Full of suspense and playfulness!

GRADE LEVEL

3–6

SKILLS PRACTICED

Focusing, self-control, mathematics

MATERIALS NEEDED

Two objects, such as balls or bean bags, of different sizes to be passed around the circle; a stopwatch or clock with a second hand

PREPARING STUDENTS FOR SUCCESS

- Discuss safely passing the balls or beanbags while doing so as fast as possible.

- Discuss "what-ifs"—what if a ball or beanbag is dropped, etc.

- Remind students that they must remain in the circle and that only one student at a time may hold a ball or beanbag.

ACTIONS

The smaller object is the bunny; the larger one is the farmer. Begin in a circle in your meeting area or around the perimeter of the classroom. Assign a student to time the chase and start the bunny around the circle. About halfway through the circle, start the farmer in the same direction. The farmer may change directions to try to catch the bunny, but the bunny may go in only one direction.

The farmer catches the bunny by touching it; this ends the first round of the game.

Repeat the game, and for each round, assign a student to time the chase. The goal is to be able to catch the bunny in the least amount of time.

Check My Beat

Here's a great one to stir children's energies while having fun playing with rhythm.

GRADE LEVEL

3–6

SKILLS PRACTICED

Self-control, rhythm, creativity

MATERIALS NEEDED

None

PREPARING STUDENTS FOR SUCCESS

This chant may be difficult for students with little exposure to rhythms, so take some time to practice together what a steady four-beat rhythm sounds like. Then brainstorm and practice some variations using any body part: hands gently slapping thighs, knees, or chest; snapping fingers; stomping feet, etc.

WORDS

Leader *Here's my rhythm, now check my beat!*
Group *We've got your rhythm, now here's your beat!*

ACTIONS

Best done in a circle but also works with children at their tables or desks; just establish a turn-taking order.

Leader Establishes a steady four-beat rhythm through clapping or light knee-slapping

Group Copies the leader

Leader Chants *Here's my rhythm, now check my beat* and creates a new clap-slap pattern

Group Chants *We've got your rhythm, now here's your beat!* and copies the leader's actions

Child 1 Chants *Here's my rhythm, now check my beat* and creates a new clap-slap pattern

Group Chants *We've got your rhythm, now here's your beat!* and copies child 1

Child 2 Chants *Here's my rhythm, now check my beat* and creates a new clap-slap pattern

Continue around the circle or the room until all have had a chance to share their clap-slap pattern. Repeats are okay!

Sample clap-slap patterns

Clap-Clap-Slap-Slap
Clap-Slap-Clap-Slap
Slap-Clap-Slap-Clap
Slap-Slap-Slap-Clap

Clapping Patterns

This simple clap and echo-clap activity offers one of the easiest ways to get a group's attention. It's a good lead-in to other energizers.

GRADE LEVEL

K–6

SKILLS PRACTICED

Focusing, listening, self-control, creativity

MATERIALS NEEDED

None

ACTIONS

Begin clapping out a rhythm that's easy to repeat and familiar to the group, for example:

Clap (rest)
Clap (rest)
Clap-clap-clap

The group will immediately echo this same clapping pattern. Do this a couple of times before changing it around a bit, for example:

Clap-clap-clap-clap (rest)
Clap-clap

Continue varying the clapping patterns as you wish. End by snapping your fingers to the original clapping pattern. The children will echo-snap and finish with being silent. For young children, end with a finger over your lips as you make the quiet sound:

Shhh
Shhh
Shhh-shhh-shhh

VARIATIONS

- Add other rhythmic body sounds—foot stomps, knee slaps, palm slides, tongue clicks, etc.

- Invite children to take turns leading the group

- Ask a music teacher for ideas

Clap Your Hands

Another simple movement game that allows young children to feel successful and energized immediately. Easy and fun to do.

GRADE LEVEL

K–3

SKILLS PRACTICED

Focusing, listening, self-control

MATERIALS NEEDED

None

PREPARING STUDENTS FOR SUCCESS

Talk with the children about ways to safely swing their arms and move around while keeping everyone safe.

WORDS AND ACTIONS

Children do each movement as they chant it.

Clap clap clap your hands
Clap your hands together!

Swing swing swing your arms
Swing your arms together!

March march march around
March around together!

Jump jump up and down
Up and down together!

Continue with various movements, working with the children's energy levels. Some possibilities:

Bend your knees
Snap your fingers
Click your tongue
Sing a song
Sit right down
Whisper softly
Shhh!

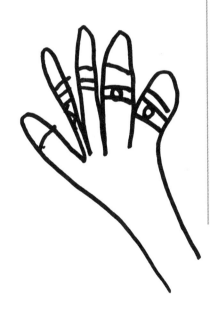

Deep and Wide

Everyone sings together, doing the motions that go with the words. The fun starts with the repeats—each time, you drop words but still do the motion that goes with each word.

GRADE LEVEL

K–3

SKILLS PRACTICED

Focusing, creativity, memory, self-control

MATERIALS NEEDED

None

PREPARING STUDENTS FOR SUCCESS

Practice the words and motions.

WORDS

Deep and wide,
Deep and wide,
There's a river flowing
Deep and wi-ide!

Deep and wide,
Deep and wide,
There's a river flowing
Deep and wide!

(repeat from beginning five times)

ACTIONS

Deep: One hand high and one hand low, as if showing depth

Wide: Right hand stretches out to the right, left hand out to the left, as if showing width

River flowing: Both hands on left and then waving gently to the right, as if showing water moving past

SEQUENCE FOR REMOVING WORDS

First repeat: Drop *deep*

Second repeat: Drop *deep* and *wide*

Third repeat: Drop *deep, wide,* and *river*

Fourth repeat: Drop *deep, wide, river,* and *flowing*

Fifth repeat: Sing the whole song again with all the words included

17

Did You Know?

A game of mis-matches and reversals that limbers up the brain.

GRADE LEVEL

3–6

SKILLS PRACTICED

Self-control, focusing, creativity

MATERIALS NEEDED

None

This one's tricky! Ask for a volunteer partner and carefully model this one for the class. Ask students what they notice, and be sure they understand the game before sending them off with their own partners.

WORDS AND ACTIONS

Here's an example:

Player 1 points to her **ear** and says, *Did you know, this is my **elbow**?*

Player 2 points to his **elbow** and says: *No! But did you know, this is my **ear**?*

Player 2 then points to his **foot** and says, *And, did you know, this is my **neck**?*

Player 1 points to her **neck** and says, *No! But did you know this is my **foot**?*

Player 1 then points to her **head** and says, *And, did you know, this is my **hand**?*

Player 2 points to his **hand** and says *No! But did you know this is my **head**?*

Player 2 then points to his **nose** and says *And, did you know, this is my **knee**?*

Player 1 points to her **knee** and says *No! But did you know this is my **nose**?*

Player 1 then points to her **ankle** and says, *And, did you know, this is my **hair**?*

Play continues in this pattern for a set time or until you signal the current player to say *And, this is the end!*

VARIATION

Try it with groups of three or four.

Dino Dinner Chant

A fun chant to use anytime, but especially when you're doing a unit on dinosaurs.

GRADE LEVEL

K–3

SKILLS PRACTICED

Rhyming, oral language, rhythm

MATERIALS NEEDED

Optional: Chart with words

PREPARING STUDENTS FOR SUCCESS

Practice saying the chant together.

WORDS AND ACTIONS

Clap hands on thighs to keep a steady beat.

__All__osaurus!

__Steg__osaurus!

__Apat__osaurus too!

They __all__ went out to __din__ner

At the __din__osaur zoo.

Al__ong__ came a __wait__er called

Ty__ran__nosaurus __Rex__

He __gob__bled up their __ta__ble

'cause they __would__n't pay their __checks__!

They __would__n't pay their __checks__!

VARIATION

Use different dinosaur names.

The Doctor Says

A creative, challenging variation on the classic game of Simon Says.

GRADE LEVEL

3–6

SKILLS PRACTICED

Comprehension, memorization, focusing, listening, self-control, empathy

MATERIALS NEEDED

List of the bones in the human body

PREPARING STUDENTS FOR SUCCESS

You can use this one as a follow-up or reinforcement to learning the scientific names for the human bones.

- Make sure students know the body parts before beginning.

- Invite students to share strategies on ways they can remember the terms.

- Talk about how to respond kindly if someone makes a mistake.

WORDS AND ACTIONS

Students quickly touch the bone you name, but only if you say *Dr. _____ says* first. If children make a mistake by touching an incorrect body part or moving when you do not say *Dr. _____ says,* they can team up with another student who may need help finding the bones.

Dr. _____ says, put your hand on your . . .

Ulna	Lower arm
Radius	Lower arm
Humerus	Upper arm
Scapula	Armpit back
Clavicle	Collar or shoulder bone
Carpals	Wrist
Cranium	Head
Patella	Knee cap
Tibia	Lower leg
Fibula	Lower leg
Pelvis	Hips
Vertebrae	Backbone
Sternum	Chest
Femur	Upper leg
Mandible	Jaw

- Have children take turns being the Doctor (and inserting their name) and leading the group through the actions.

- Give each student one turn to name a part of the body to touch, going around the classroom student by student.

- Challenge the class by seeing if everyone can name and correctly identify one different body part.

Double This Double That

A partner clapping game.

GRADE LEVEL

3–6

SKILLS PRACTICED

Memorization, oral language, rhythm, self-control, creativity, empathy, cooperation

MATERIALS NEEDED

Optional: Chart with words

PREPARING STUDENTS FOR SUCCESS

■ Practice saying the chant together.

■ Model and practice actions for each motion with a partner, emphasizing that all motions need to be gentle.

■ Begin slowly!

■ Talk about respectful ways to support partners who need help learning the words and motions.

WORDS AND ACTIONS

Hold hands in loose fists up in front of you at about chin level.

Double Double Tap pinkie side of fists twice against pinkie side of partner's fists.

This This! Tap palms twice against partner's palms.

Double Double Tap pinkie side of fists twice against pinkie side of partner's fists.

That That! Tap back of hands twice against back of partner's hands.

Double This! Tap fists once against partner's fists and then palms once against partner's palms.

Double That! Tap fists once against partner's fists and then back of hands once against back of partner's hands.

Double Double Tap pinkie side of fists twice against pinkie side of partner's fists.

This That! Tap palms once against partner's palms and then tap back of hands once against back of partner's hands.

VARIATIONS

■ Children sit facing each other in two circles, one inside the other. Each time the children repeat the chant, the inner circle moves one space to the right so that each child gets a new partner.

■ Play without sound when you need a quiet waiting game.

Do What I Said, Not What I Say

This one really makes you listen!

GRADE LEVEL

3–6

SKILLS PRACTICED

Concentration, self-control, listening, memory, coordination

MATERIALS NEEDED

None

PREPARING STUDENTS FOR SUCCESS

Practice until all the children understand the concept of doing the previously mentioned action.

WORDS AND ACTIONS

Stand facing the children and call out a command. Students must follow the previously given command, not the immediate one. For example:

Leader *Stand on one foot!*
Students do nothing.

Leader *Hop on one foot!*
Students stand on one foot.

Leader *Flap your arms!*
Students hop on one foot.

Leader *Pat your head!*
Students flap their arms.

Leader *Sit down!*
Students pat their heads.

Leader *Fold your hands on your desks!*
Students sit down.

Leader *Fold your hands on your desks!*
Students fold their hands on their desks and are ready for the next lesson or activity of the day.

VARIATION

To add more challenge, the leader may pantomime the motion as well as say it.

Dum Dum Dah Dah

A follow-the-leader movement activity. Players chant or sing *Dum Dum Dah Dah* as they make the motions.

GRADE LEVEL

K–6

SKILLS PRACTICED

Rhyming, oral language, rhythm, self-control, creativity

MATERIALS NEEDED

None

PREPARING STUDENTS FOR SUCCESS

- If necessary, discuss the meaning of the word "echo."

- Share ways to maintain self-control while staying in one place.

WORDS AND ACTIONS

Children simply repeat your words and actions. Vary your movements by starting off at a low energy level, moving up to medium, and then on to high. Then transition back down through the energy levels in reverse, finally ending with very calm movements. Whispering or even mouthing the words is a great way to end.

Leader

Dum Dum
Clap thighs

Dah Dah
Clap hands

Group

Dum Dum
Clap thighs

Dah Dah
Clap hands

Repeat as many times as you wish.

Possible Movements

Touching toes, reaching far to right and then left, nodding head up and down or side to side, snapping fingers, reaching forwards and then behind back, reaching up high, bending at waist, moving knees up and down as if marching, doing jumping jacks, making large arms circles, jumping high and then touching ground

Ending

Hum instead of saying the words, then whisper the words, and finish with *shh shh shh shh!*

VARIATIONS

- Do slow, fast, loud, soft, whisper.

- Invite students to lead when you feel they're ready.

Dum   dum   dah   dah!   Dum   dum   dah   dah!

23 The Fidget Family

Good games last forever—this one dates back to the 1800s. It's acquired a few modern twists since then.

GRADE LEVEL

K–3

SKILLS PRACTICED

Focusing, listening, self-control

MATERIALS NEEDED

None

PREPARING STUDENTS FOR SUCCESS

- Practice safely standing and twirling and then carefully sitting back down.

- Share strategies on how to listen for your part—the story moves quickly!

WORDS

Once upon a time, there was a family called The Fidget Family. There were lots of people in this family. There were Ma Fidget, Pa Fidget, Billy Fidget, Tommy Fidget, Bridget Fidget, and Baby Fidget. They had several pets. They had a cat, a dog, a canary, and two horses named Old Mol and Old Dol. Through the gate, past a tree, and down the road in another house lived Grandma and Grandpa Fidget. One day, the whole Fidget Family decided to go visit Grandma and Grandpa Fidget at their house through the gate, past the tree, and down the road. Billy wanted to bring the cat, Tommy wanted to bring the dog, and Bridget wanted to bring the canary, but Ma and Pa Fidget said no. The baby cried. So they loaded up the wagon, hitched up Old Mol and Old Dol, and headed out through the gate, past the tree, and down the road to Grandma and Grandpa Fidget's house. They had just passed the tree when the baby cried again and they all realized they'd left the baby's blanket back

at the house. The baby kept crying. So, the whole Fidget Family turned the wagon around, and Old Mol and Old Dol pulled the wagon back up the road, past the tree, and through the gate. They finally found the baby's blanket back at the house. Before they left, Billy asked if he could bring the cat, Tommy wanted to bring the dog, and Bridget wanted to bring the canary, but Ma and Pa Fidget said no. The baby started chewing on the blanket. Then, the whole family got back into the wagon being pulled by Old Mol and Old Dol. They rode out through the gate, past the tree, and down the road to Grandma and Grandpa Fidget's house. They had a wonderful time, and the whole Fidget Family lived happily ever after!

ACTIONS

Students are assigned different roles from the story, which you then read aloud. When a child hears her part read, she stands up, twirls around once, and sits back down. When you read the phrase *the Fidget Family*, everyone stands, twirls around once, and sits back down.

Roles for a class of nineteen: Ma, Pa, Billy, Tommy, Bridget, Baby, Grandma, Grandpa, Old Mol, Old Dol, cat, dog, canary, wagon, house, road, tree, gate, blanket.

Delete or add characters as necessary. For more than nineteen players, you can either add more characters or assign more players to one character. Remember to adjust the story as necessary to fit your characters!

VARIATION

Invite students to write their own Fidget Family stories with their own invented characters.

Five Plump Peas

A fun finger play and a nice accompaniment for any garden or nutrition unit.

GRADE LEVEL

K–3

SKILLS PRACTICED

Focusing, listening, self-control

MATERIALS NEEDED

None

PREPARING STUDENTS FOR SUCCESS

- Practice the words first, without the movements.

- When you're ready to play, make sure children have enough room to spread their arms out safely.

- Practice a loud, safe clap.

WORDS AND ACTIONS

Five** plump **peas
*in a **pea**pod **pressed**.*
Hands in fists, knuckles pressed together

***One** grew*
Straighten thumbs and touch tips together

***two** grew,*
Straighten pointer fingers and touch tips together

***So** did the **rest**!*
Straighten all other fingers and press palms together

*And they **grew** and they **grew***
Begin to move hands apart

*and they **never stopped***
*and they **grew** so **big***
*that the **pea**pod ...*

Keep moving hands apart until they're stretched out as far as possible, making voice sound as if it's really hard work. Pause dramatically after you say *peapod*.

***popped**!*
Clap loudly!

Froggie

Great to incorporate into those spring pond units. A companion piece to "Mosquito" (number 44).

GRADE LEVEL

K–6

SKILLS PRACTICED

Focusing, listening, self-control

MATERIALS NEEDED

None

WORDS AND ACTIONS

Keep a steady beat by alternately clapping hands against thighs and then clapping hands together. The leader calls out each line, which the group then repeats.

Dog!
Dog—Cat!
Dog—Cat—Mouse!
Froggie*!*
Itsy bitsy **teen**y weenie **tiny** little **frog**gie
Jump …, jump, jump, **jump** little **frog**gie
Eating up **all** the **bugs** and little **spi**ders
Fleas and **flies** are **scrump**dillyicious
Ribbit ribbit **rib**bit ribbit **rib**bit ribbit **croak***!*

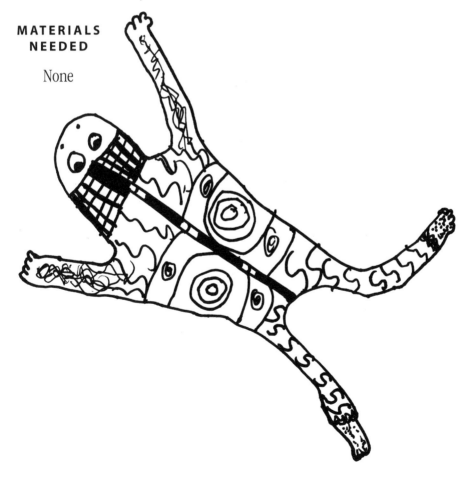

26 # Funga Alafia

A lovely song of welcome from West Africa. The words and gestures mean, roughly, "I welcome you with my thoughts, my words, and my open heart—see, I have nothing up my sleeves! May peace be with you."

PRONUNCIATION

Funga: **foon**-gă

Alafia: ah-**lă**-fē-ah

Ahshay: ă-**shā**

GRADE LEVEL

K–6

SKILLS PRACTICED

Cooperation, language arts, cultural awareness

MATERIALS NEEDED

Song chart

PREPARING STUDENTS FOR SUCCESS

1. Show the children the song chart. Invite a conversation about ways people welcome each other, and say that this is a special welcoming song used in many places in Africa.

2. Read the words together, making sure children understand the pronunciation and the simple welcoming meaning of the words.

3. Sing the song through once, without any motions. Have the children practice singing the tune.

4. Last, teach the motions, explain the meaning of each, and invite the children to join in singing and motioning.

WORDS

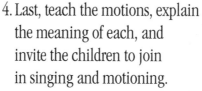

Funga Alafia
Ah-shay Ah-shay!

Funga Alafia
Ah-shay Ah-shay!

ACTIONS

The song is sung four times through, each time adding a new movement for the Funga Alafia portion. The Ah-shay Ah-shay portion is always the same: arms extended with palms upright. When doing all these motions, move to the beat with a gentle, steady up-and-down or back-and-forth motion.

First time through—point to your forehead

Second time through—point to your mouth

Third time through—cross your hands over your heart

Fourth time through—bend your arms at the elbows in front of you. Move your arms back and forth as if you were gently slipping your arms up your sleeves or rubbing your forearms

VARIATION

Sing as a round or with harmonies—enjoy experimenting with this one!

Fun-ga Al-a-fia, Ah-shay Ah-shay, Fun-ga Al-a-fia, Ah-shay Ah-shay. Ah-shay Ah-shay!

*upper octave optional

Go Bananas

A favorite among students and teachers alike. Use to accompany a unit on nutrition, or when you just feel the need to be a little silly.

GRADE LEVEL

K–3

SKILLS PRACTICED

Rhyming, oral language, rhythm, self-control, left and right, creativity

MATERIALS NEEDED

Optional: Chart with words

PREPARING STUDENTS FOR SUCCESS

- Practice saying the chant together.

- Model and practice actions for each movement; specifically, make sure each child has room to do a standing split at the end.

- Share ways to maintain self-control while staying in one place.

WORDS AND ACTIONS

Bananas

*Bananas…**Unite**!*
While standing, extend arms upward, palms together over head

Peel bananas
Peel-peel bananas
Wiggle left arm down along left side of body

Peel bananas
Peel-peel bananas
Wiggle right arm down along right side of body

Peel them to the left
Swing left arm up and behind head

Peel them to the right
Swing right arm up and behind head

Peel them down the middle
Swing both arms down in front and then out to sides

And Unh! Take a bite
Pull both fists down hard at sides while bending knees

And Unh! Take a bite

Pull both fists down hard at sides while bending knees

Go bananas
Point both index fingers up and down above head while slowly twirling in a circle

Go-go bananas
Continue pointing and twirling

Go bananas
Continue pointing and twirling

Go-go bananas
Continue pointing and twirling

*Bananas … **Split**!*
Raise arms straight up and then do a standing split—one arm and leg stretched forward, the other arm and leg stretched backward—FREEZE!

VARIATIONS

Use during transitions, such as from circle to group areas. When you get to *Bananas … **Split**!* at the end, replace the word "bananas" with four to five children's names that will be moving out of the group to their next area. Then repeat the chant with those remaining in the circle until all children have been dismissed.

OTHER VERSIONS

These versions are rhythmically similar to the banana version but omit the movements to the right, left, and middle.

Popcorn	Potato	Orange
Form the corn *Form-form the corn* Stand up straight, raise arms, and clasp hands above head	*Form the potato* *Form-form the potato* Start standing and slowly squat down low, curling into a round potato-like figure	*Form the orange* *Form-form the orange* While standing, hold arms out in front, rounded as if encircling a giant orange
Shuck the corn *Shuck-shuck the corn* Wiggle and lower arms slowly down one at a time	*Grate the potato* *Grate-grate the potato* Scrape right hand twice against left arm and then left hand twice against right arm	*Peel the orange* *Peel-peel the orange* Pull one arm and then the other slowly back
Pop the corn *Pop-pop the corn* Jump up and down	*Mash the potato* *Mash-mash the potato* Stamp feet while slowly standing and tapping one fist atop the other	*Squeeze the orange* *Squeeze-squeeze the orange* Hug yourself

Granny at the Fair

A variation of
"My Sweet Old
Aunt" with another
fun ending.

GRADE LEVEL

K–3

**SKILLS
PRACTICED**

Self-control,
creativity

**MATERIALS
NEEDED**

Optional:
A chart with
the words

WORDS AND ACTIONS

Children stand up and join in chanting and doing the
motions.

My granny went to the county fair.
And she bought a drum while she was there.
And she drummed, and she drummed
And she drummed, and she drummed
Pretend to play the drums

My granny went to the county fair.
And she bought a fan while she was there.
And she fanned, and she fanned
And she fanned, and she fanned
Fan self with left hand

And she drummed …
Pretend to play a drum

My granny went to the county fair
And she bought some shears while she was there
And she cut, and she cut
And she cut, and she cut
Pretend to cut with right hand

And she fanned …
Fan self with left hand

And she drummed …
Pretend to play a drum

My granny went to the county fair.
And she bought some gum while she was there.
And she chewed, and she chewed
And she chewed, and she chewed
Pretend to chew gum

And she cut…
Pretend to cut with right hand

And she fanned…
Fan self with left hand

And she drummed…
Pretend to play a drum

My granny went to the county fair.
And she blew a bubble while she was there.
And she blew, and she blew
And she blew, and she blew
Hold hands palms together in front of mouth and pretend to blow a bubble,
moving hands wider apart with each *blew* to show the bubble growing larger
and larger

*And she blew, and **pop**!*
Clap hands loudly!

29 Hand Dance

Don't have enough room for a dance floor? Try hand dancing at your seats for the same festive effect.

GRADE LEVEL

K–6

SKILLS PRACTICED

Self-control, creativity

MATERIALS NEEDED

Some lively music

PREPARING STUDENTS FOR SUCCESS

Model self-control skills of staying in your space while hand dancing.

WORDS AND ACTIONS

Children begin sitting, either on the floor or at their seats. Turn on the music and announce, *It's time for the hand dance!* Then do each dance motion for fifteen to thirty seconds as the children follow along and join in the fun.

Do the Monkey!
Put fists out in front and pretend to climb a vine.

Do the Pony!
Pretend to hold reins and bounce up and down.

Do the Swim!
Move arms as if swimming.

Do the Hitchhike!
Stick up thumbs and move them back and forth in front of body.

Do the Twist!
Bend elbows and twist body at waist.

Do the Funky Chicken!
Make arms like wings and flap up and down.

Do the Batman!
Make V's with fingers and sweep in front of eyes.

- After the children learn all the hand dances, invite them to make the selections. You choose the first dance. Then when it's time to change, nod your head to the next student, who then announces the next hand dance. Continue in this way around the room.

- Invite children to make up their own hand dances and teach them to the class.

30 Have a Ball

You may see children mischievously tossing paper. Here's a structured way for them to do so while strengthening their abdominal muscles (among others).

GRADE LEVEL

3–6

SKILLS PRACTICED

Self-control, coordination

MATERIALS NEEDED

Scrap paper

PREPARING STUDENTS FOR SUCCESS

Do careful modeling and clarifying of expectations as to what happens with the paper balls.

ACTIONS

Begin by having students wad up a piece of paper to make a ball. Challenge the students to balance and move their ball in these ways:

- Place the ball on your feet (feet together) while seated and repeatedly toss up and catch the ball with the top of your feet (as in hacky sack).

- Set the ball on an elbow. Flip the ball into the air and catch it with the hand on the same side.

- Lift the legs off the floor (feet together). Starting with the ball in the right hand, pass it under your legs to the left hand, over your legs to the right hand, and so on.

- With your hands, toss the ball backwards over your head and move your hands behind your back to catch it.

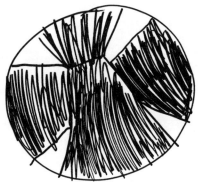

- Lift the legs (feet slightly apart) and use first one hand and then the other as you weave the ball between the left and right legs in a figure eight pattern. For example, starting with the right hand, pass the ball over your right leg. Reach under your left leg to take the ball with your left hand. Now, with your left hand, pass the ball over your left leg and reach under your right leg to take the ball with your right hand. Continue in this pattern.

- Toss the ball from behind the back and catch in the front.

- While standing, circle the waist with the ball, passing the ball from hand to hand as you go.

VARIATION

Allow students to shoot their ball into the recycle bin at the end. If some miss, they simply pick up their ball and place it in the bin.

Head, Shoulders, Knees & Toes

An old favorite with a few new ingredients.

GRADE LEVEL

K–3

SKILLS PRACTICED

Self-control, balance, coordination

MATERIALS NEEDED

None

PREPARING STUDENTS FOR SUCCESS

Discuss and practice ways to be safe while moving quickly.

WORDS AND ACTIONS

Sing the words while placing hands on each part of the body as it's named.

Head, shoulders, knees and toes
Knees and toes
Head, shoulders, knees and toes
Knees and toes … and …
Eyes and ears and mouth and nose
Head, shoulders, knees and toes
Knees and toes!

Ankles, elbows, feet and seat
Feet and seat
Ankles, elbows, feet and seat
Feet and seat … and …
Hair and hips and chin and cheeks
Ankles, elbows, feet and seat
Feet and seat!

VARIATIONS

■ Try this muscle verse, posing like a body builder. Remember to teach the muscle locations first.

—*Original by the author*

Biceps, triceps, quads and glutes
Quads and glutes
Biceps, triceps, quads and glutes
Quads and glutes … and …

Pecs and lats and abs and calves
Biceps, triceps, quads and glutes
Quads and glutes!!!

  Biceps: Top of the upper arm
  Triceps: Bottom of the upper arm
  Quads: Front of thigh
  Glutes: Bottom
  Pecs: Chest
  Lats: Middle of the back
  Abs: Stomach

- Make up new verses for other themes;
  for example, bones (cranium, sternum,
  pelvis, and clavicle) or winter clothing (hat,
  earmuffs, scarf, and gloves).

- When the children become very familiar with a particular verse, try singing
  it backwards.

- Repeat the chant several times, each time chanting faster.

- Give the children a choice of chanting at a different speed on each repeat:
  super slow, slow, medium, fast, or super fast.

32 High Low Up & Down

Very simple but catchy tune that invites word play.

GRADE LEVEL

K–3

SKILLS PRACTICED

Focusing, listening, self-control, creativity

MATERIALS NEEDED

None

Leader sings or chants:
High low
Up and down
Can your voice
make this sound?

Leader in a high voice:
La la la!
Group echoes

Leader in a low voice:
Ugh ugh ugh!
Group echoes

Leader then repeats the "High low" verse, offering more sounds for the group to echo. For example:

Possible high/low pairs:

meow, ruff
beep, boom
eep, oop
goo, ga
ooh, aah

High, low, up and down! Can your voice make this sound?

Hot Tamale

An all-over-the-body version of Hot Potato. Children stay in place while doing each movement.

GRADE LEVEL

K–6

SKILLS PRACTICED

Self-control, balance, coordination

MATERIALS NEEDED

Optional—a chart or overhead with directions for the movements

PREPARING STUDENTS FOR SUCCESS

■ If necessary, tell the children what a tamale is.

■ Talk about making safe movements while staying in their own space.

WORDS AND ACTIONS

Playfully tell the children:

There's a hot tamale right next to you! Watch out—it moves! And I as your leader know just where it is, so I'll take care of you by telling you which direction to move so you won't get scorched. Here we go!

Now excitedly call out movements for the children to do:

Move backward!
Back stroke (swimming motion)

Up higher!
Make ladder-climbing motion

Bend down low!
Squat down

Move forward!
March in place

Move to the left! [or right]
Side stretch to the left [or right]

You're practically on top of the tamale!
While staying in place, students pretend they're stepping on something hot

VARIATION

Do silently with the leader pointing to the directions on the chart.

Human Protractor

A simple yet powerful learning tool and energizer to reinforce math concepts.

GRADE LEVEL

K–6

SKILLS PRACTICED

Focusing, listening, self-control, math

MATERIALS NEEDED

None

ACTIONS

Begin with everyone standing, arms stretched straight up in the air. Then have the group touch their toes. Tell the children they're going to straighten up gradually, keeping their arms straight out in front of their bodies. At the same time, you'll be calling out numbers between 1 and 20. When you reach 20, the children's arms will again be straight up in the air. Tell the children to try to remember where their hands and arms are for each number.

Now randomly call out numbers between 1 and 20 as the children raise their bodies to roughly the same position they used for each number the first time through.

When the children are confident with the activity, invite one of them to lead it.

VARIATIONS

- Depending on your grade level and math curriculum, vary the numbers used or the digits or math problems you call out. You can use any number range for your human protractor—1 through 10, 1 through 20, 1 through 100 (count by tens for this one), or even 1 through 180, like a real protractor.

- Incorporate math problems. For example, call out a simple addition: 7+7. After the group has assumed the number position, ask one child for the answer and then have the group repeat it.

- For more challenging math problems, such as 3 × 24, or the square root of 81, or ¾ + ½, have children pair up and agree on their answer before assuming the number position.

Note: If you decide to do math problems, remember energizers are intended to be playful and fun, so don't get too caught up in the problem-solving process. Be sure to include easy problems or call out plain old numbers in between the problems.

I Feel the Same Way

A great improv activity.

GRADE LEVEL

3–6

SKILLS PRACTICED

Self-control, creativity, drama, risk-taking

MATERIALS NEEDED

Chime or other auditory signal

PREPARING STUDENTS FOR SUCCESS

- Try this one after your class has developed a strong sense of safety and community.

- Brainstorm emotions with the children and practice making the faces that go with them.

- Remind the children about maintaining the spirit of being creative in front of each other: Ask them for ideas about how we can laugh together without laughing at each other.

ACTIONS

Pair up the students and have them stand facing each other. One student begins by thinking of an emotion and then expressing that emotion through tone of voice, facial expression, and nonsense talk—just sounds, no real words.

The partner immediately begins imitating that emotion with his or her own tone, facial expression, and nonsense talk. Children needn't copy the exact nonsense talk—just express the same emotion.

At the sound of the chime, players switch roles and repeat the cycle, talking nonsense with a new emotion. Once the nonsense gets going, no pausing allowed! When you've decided they've had enough, signal for the current players to pantomime closing their eyes and going to sleep. Their partners imitate them and the game is over.

36 Imagine This

A refreshing energizer that's all about slowly building an image in your mind.

GRADE LEVEL

3–6

SKILLS PRACTICED

Self-control, creativity, visualization

MATERIALS NEEDED

None

PREPARING STUDENTS FOR SUCCESS

- Discuss what it means to imagine scenes in your mind.

- Share strategies for how to keep your eyes closed. Make closing eyes a choice if it's too uncomfortable for some, but encourage children to try it.

WORDS AND ACTIONS

Children simply sit, close their eyes, and imagine the scene in their minds. The leader begins by saying *Imagine this* and naming an object, such as a pine tree. The next person then adds a detail that she's actually imagining, such as a blue jay on the pine tree. The next player adds another detail, such as rain falling on the pine tree and blue jay, and so on. This is not a memory game necessarily, so players do not have to list all the things others have mentioned. Nor do players need to tell a story; they simply state what they're imagining.

Interruptions

This fun energizer can serve double-duty by reinforcing language arts skills.

GRADE LEVEL

K–3

SKILLS PRACTICED

Focusing, self-control, phonetic auditory awareness, sentence structure

MATERIALS NEEDED

A short passage or poem or a paragraph or two from any book the class is reading

PREPARING STUDENTS FOR SUCCESS

When introducing this energizer, start with one or two parameters and gradually add more.

ACTIONS

Clap when they hear a word that starts with the "s" sound (or another consonant sound you identify).

Snap when they hear the long "e" sound (or another vowel sound you identify).

Sit down when they hear the end of a sentence.

Stand up when they hear the beginning of a sentence.

VARIATIONS

■ Have everyone read the passage together.

■ Have students make sounds for each type of ending punctuation. For example, students could say *shoom-bop* for exclamation points, *hmmmm?* for question marks, and *zip* for periods.

38 Laughing Handkerchief

Laughter is a great relaxer—and it's wonderful to hear a group of children laughing out loud together!

GRADE LEVEL

K–6

SKILLS PRACTICED

Self-control, observation, focusing

MATERIALS NEEDED

A handkerchief (clean!), a blown-up balloon, or some other soft, lightweight object that can be easily tossed in the air

PREPARING STUDENTS FOR SUCCESS

Talk about an appropriate noise level for the classroom, and practice controlling voice volume before beginning the game.

ACTIONS

Throw a handkerchief high into the air. While it's in the air, everyone laughs. As soon as it touches the ground, everyone goes silent.

VARIATIONS

- Add other actions when the handkerchief is up in the air, such as clapping, talking, singing, etc.

- Ask the children for their ideas.

"Engaging the body and mind in physical activity during transition times will provide students with a much-needed break from sedentary time and assist them in focusing on the next learning activity."

—National Association for Sport and Physical Education

39 Left and Right

Try this one in a large circle with one or more balls, or in various small groups with one or two balls each. You'll need at least four people in a group.

GRADE LEVEL

3–6

SKILLS PRACTICED

Focusing, listening, self-control, empathy

MATERIALS NEEDED

A few bean bags, Kooshes, or other soft balls

PREPARING STUDENTS FOR SUCCESS

- Practice concepts of left and right, if the children have not already mastered them.

- Discuss what might be a friendly thing to do or say if someone makes a mistake.

WORDS AND ACTIONS

As the leader reads the story out loud, she passes the ball to her left when she first says the word "left." Thereafter, each time the leader says **left** or **right**, the person holding the ball passes it to the person to their left or right. The ball thus keeps moving from person to person as long as the game continues.

*This morning I **left** my house and was on my way to walk to school, but I **left** my homework at home, **right** by the phone!*

*I knew **right** away that I needed to have the **right** homework to turn in to my teacher, so I turned **left** and I turned **right** and I made my way back to my house for the **right** homework.*

*Finally I was back on the **right** track. I arrived at school **right** on time! Luckily I had not **left** my lunch money behind.*

*There were friends on my **right** and friends on my **left**. The homework basket was to the **left** of the door, with a* *pencil **right** next to it. I checked in, signed up for the **right** kind of lunch, and **right** away headed over to Morning Meeting.*

*We got going **right** away with a new greeting we had learned yesterday, starting where we had **left** off, and then moved **right** on to sharing. We played the **left** and **right** game and then went **right** on to our Morning Message. We talked about the **right** recycling project for our class and what choices were still **left**. And, with only two minutes **left**, we knew we had to get in line for the bus for our field trip to the Recycle Center, or else we would be **left** behind. We all marched down the hallway, pretending to be in a whispering marching band: **Left** ... **left** ... **left**, **right**, **left**! ... **Left** ... **left** ... **left**, **right**, **left**!*

*We had so much fun at our field trip, and learned lots about the **right** way to recycle and take care of our planet.*

*So if you want to be a responsible citizen and take care of our environment, make sure you help each other make the **right** decisions. Don't get **left** behind! You can jump **right** in and make the **right** decision to save our planet.*

*And with that, there is nothing **left** for me to say, so ... congratulations to our friends! They are patiently sitting just to the **left** of you!*

VARIATIONS

- Instead of circling up and passing a ball, simply have the children stand at their desks. On the words *left* or *right*, children move to the desk at their left or right.

- Make up your own left and right stories with the children.

- The leader begins a left and right story. After a few sentences, whoever has the ball continues the story for a few more sentences. If the story goes on and on, simply tell the next child or two that they must complete the story, or we'll be **left** here all day!

40 Let's Get the Rhythm

A basic chant that's good as an introduction to other chants. Also helpful to do with a small group of children who are waiting at the circle for the rest of the class to join them. Children can easily join in the chant whenever they arrive in the circle.

GRADE LEVEL

K–3

SKILLS PRACTICED

Focusing, listening, self-control

MATERIALS NEEDED

None

PREPARING STUDENTS FOR SUCCESS

Practice saying the words and doing the actions together. Before you begin chanting as a group, establish the rhythm by tapping your own knees a few times as the children watch.

WORDS

Throughout the chant, continue tapping knees to the rhythm. You'll replace the body part named and the bracketed words with each verse.

Let's** get the **rhythm** of our **knees

Let's** get the **rhythm** of our **knees

***Let's** get the **rhythm** of our **knees** [if you please!]*

Let's** get the **rhythm** of our **knees

Continue chanting and tapping hands rhythmically on the following body parts. Replace the bracketed words in the knees verse with the bracketed words listed for each body part.

Shoulders—[Big boulders!]
Head—[Oh, dread!]
Feet—[How neat!]
Belly—[Jelly belly!]

VARIATION

Invite the children to choose body parts and rhymes to go with them.

41 # Lyle Crocodile

A great movement activity to accompany any unit on the rainforest, the Nile River, or crocodile stories or to make a fun connection for children studying the number 100.

—*Original by the author*

GRADE LEVEL

K–3

SKILLS PRACTICED

Focusing, listening, self-control

MATERIALS NEEDED

None

WORDS AND ACTIONS

Lyle Lyle
Crocodile!
***Swam** the **Nile** for **100** miles!*
Clap a steady beat on thighs

Swim
Swim
Swim-swim-swim!
Swim
Swim
Swim-swim-swim!
Pantomime swimming

Continue repeating the words, changing the third line and the pantomime with each repeat:

***Clapped** his **hands** for **100** miles!*
***Twirled** on his **tail** for **100** miles!*
***Snapped** his **fingers** for **100** miles!*
***Chomped** his **teeth** for **100** miles!*

Second-to-last verse:

Lyle Lyle
Crocodile!
Went to sleep for 100 miles!
Snee
Snore
Snee-snee-snore!
Snee
Snore
Snee-snee-snore!

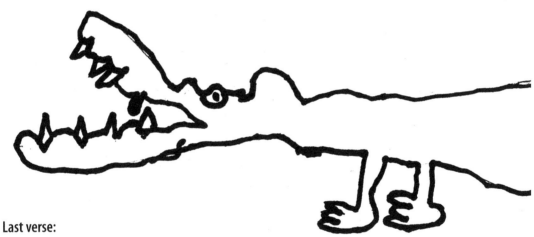

Last verse:

Lyle's all done
He's had his fun!
Tomorrow he'll do
One hundred and one!!!
Hold up pointer fingers one at a time to go along with *one hundred and one*.

42 Ma Zinga!

A great community builder that you can use either to motivate or celebrate.

GRADE LEVEL

K–6

SKILLS PRACTICED

Focusing, listening, self-control, empathy, assertion

MATERIALS NEEDED

None

WORDS

Ma-a-a-a-a-a-a…
Zinga!!!

ACTIONS

Choose a leader. Stand together in a circle, with everyone's arms pointing straight into the middle of the circle.

The group begins to say and hold the sound *Ma-a-a-a …*, building up spirit and positive energy. At the leader's signal— a nod of the head—the group quickly pulls back their hands while forming fists, bending their elbows back and cheering together loudly, **Zinga!!!** This pulls all that great group energy back to each individual. Repeat, inviting students to take turns being the leader.

Mirrors

Creativity and control are keys to success in this calming activity. Younger children may also enjoy it if supported with clear, explicit directions and simple movement examples.

GRADE LEVEL

3–6

SKILLS PRACTICED

Observation, focusing, creativity, self-control

MATERIALS NEEDED

A chime or some other type of gentle auditory signal

PREPARING STUDENTS FOR SUCCESS

Brainstorm and practice various movements that can be done slowly and steadily. Remind students to move at a slow pace, and challenge them to synchronize their movements with their partner's. Ask students to share strategies for doing this successfully.

ACTIONS

Students stand and select a nearby partner (or you may assign partners). Partners decide who'll be the leader first, and that student begins making slow and steady movements. The follower mirrors the leader's motions.

At the teacher's signal, the two switch roles.

VARIATIONS

- Choose one student to lead the class. After a few motions, the leader passes the lead to another classmate by pointing to her or him.

- Have two groups of partners join each other. One pair does the mirroring activity while the other watches and works together to guess who the leader is.

"Actively experiencing the rhythm of words and sentences helps children find the rhythm necessary for reading and writing. Whether children are clapping or tapping out the beat of a fingerplay or moving to the cadence of a poem, they hear and feel the rhythm of words."

—Rae Pica, children's physical activity specialist

Mosquito

A companion piece to "Froggie" (number 25).

GRADE LEVEL

K–6

SKILLS PRACTICED

Focusing, listening, self-control

MATERIALS NEEDED

None

WORDS AND ACTIONS

Keep a steady beat by alternately clapping hands against thighs and then clapping hands together. The leader calls out each line, which the group then repeats.

Flea!
Flea-Fly!
*Flea-Fly-**Mosquito**!*
***Oh**-no no **no** more mos**qui**toes!*
***Itchy** itchy **scratchy** scratchy—**ewww I** got one **down** my backy!*

Ending:

***Get** that **big** bad **bug** with the **bug** spray!*
Pantomime holding a can of bug spray
Pppsssshhhhhhh!!
***Smack**!*
Clap loudly

Alternate ending:

***Get** me **my** pink **cal**amine **lo**tion!*
Pantomime holding up a bottle
*AHHHHHHH—**All bet**ter!*
Rub arms and back while smiling

Mumbo Jumbo Bubblegum

A just-for-fun chant.

GRADE LEVEL
K–3

SKILLS PRACTICED

Rhyming, oral language, rhythm

MATERIALS NEEDED

Optional:
Chart with words

PREPARING STUDENTS FOR SUCCESS

Teach and practice this one in four steps:

- Words
- Words with rhythmic clapping
- Pantomime
- Words, rhythmic clapping, and pantomime all together.

WORDS AND ACTIONS

1. Chant the following words while clapping hands on thighs to keep a steady beat.

   Mumbo Jumbo
   Christopher Columbo
   Sitting on the sidewalk
   Chewing bubble-gumbo!
   Clap hands on thighs to keep a steady beat.

2. While continuing to clap hands on thighs, pantomime chewing bubblegum, rhythmically and with sound effects:

   Chomp … chomp
   Chomp-chomp-chomp!

3. Repeat 1 and 2, this time saying the words and making the sounds a little louder.

4. Repeat 1 and 2, this time making sounds as if your mouth is too full of bubblegum.

5. After the last "chomp," pause, stop clapping hands against thighs, take a deep breath, and begin blowing a bubble. With each of four puffs, move your hands apart in front of your face to mimic a bubble that gets larger with each puff. On "SMACK," clap your hands together loudly as if the bubble has popped.

Foo ... foo
Foo ... foo **SMACK***!!!*

VARIATION

Follow up this chant with any bubble gum song, such as "Sticky Sticky Bubblegum" or "Bazooka-zooka Bubblegum."

My Bonny

An old favorite song with a twist. Can you keep up?

GRADE LEVEL

K–3

SKILLS PRACTICED

Focusing, listening, self-control, recognition of letter sounds, reading (for younger children)

MATERIALS NEEDED

For younger children, a chart with words

PREPARING STUDENTS FOR SUCCESS

■ For the first few times, simply teach the words and tune of the song. (Remember, just singing together can be very energizing!) Once the students are comfortable with the song, introduce the movements.

■ Do some teaching on the meaning of the word "Bonny."

WORDS AND ACTIONS

Begin with everyone seated. Children stand on the first "b" word, sit on the second, and continue reversing positions throughout the song.

My Bonny lies over the ocean
My Bonny lies over the sea
My Bonny lies over the ocean
So bring back my Bonny to me.

Bring back,
Bring back,
Oh bring back my Bonny to me, to me.
Bring back,
Bring back,
Oh bring back my Bonny to me.

VARIATION

■ Count off the class by twos. Have the ones begin by sitting, and the twos begin by standing. Then watch and enjoy as the class bobs up and down opposite one another.

■ Once children know the verse well, use it to play "Interruptions" (number 37).

My Favorite Sport

This energizer is a wonderful companion to any sports curriculum or time of year when sports are prevalent in the community. —*Original by the author*

GRADE LEVEL

K–6

SKILLS PRACTICED

Rhyming, oral language, rhythm, self-control, creativity

MATERIALS NEEDED

Optional: Chart with words

PREPARING STUDENTS FOR SUCCESS

- Teach and practice the chant first, then the actions, and then the chant and actions together.
- Share ways to maintain self-control while staying in one place.

WORDS

To begin all verses, stand and bend slightly from the waist.

Basketball

***Bas**ketball is my **fav**orite **sport**
I **love** to **drib**ble up and **down** the **court***
On the beats, alternately clap hands together and then against thighs

Dribble!
Dribble!
Pantomime dribbling a basketball

*Dribble-dribble—**Shoot**!*
Pantomime dribbling and then shooting a basket

Dribble!
Dribble!
Pantomime dribbling a basketball

*Dribble-dribble—**Shoot**!*
Pantomime dribbling and then shooting a basket

Baseball

*The **base**ball field is my **fav**orite **place**
I **love** to run **fast** over **every** **base***
On the beats, alternately clap hands together and then against thighs

My Favorite Sport, cont.

Run!
Run!
Pantomime running in place

*Run-run—**Slide**!*
Pantomime a standing slide into a base

Run!
Run!
Pantomime running in place

*Run-run—**Slide**!*
Pantomime a standing slide into a base

Hockey

*The **hockey rink** is really **nice***
*I **love** to pass the **puck** all **over** the **ice***
On the beats, alternately clap hands together and then against thighs

Pass!
Pass!
Pantomime passing puck to right or left

*Pass-pass—**Goal**!*
Pantomime passing and then sweeping puck forward

Pass!
Pass!
Pantomime passing puck to right or left

*Pass-pass—**Goal**!*
Pantomime passing and then sweeping puck forward

Dog Sledding

Dog** sledding **is** the **way** to **go
*I **love** to mush the **dog** team **over** the **snow***
On the beats, alternately clap hands together and then against thighs

Mush! Mush!
Pantomime holding onto sled handle and weaving back and forth

*Mush-mush—**Whoa**!*
Pull hands back while leaning back a little

Mush! Mush!
Pantomime holding onto sled handle and weaving back and forth

*Mush-mush—**Whoa**!*
Pull hands back while leaning back a little

Swimming

Do**ing the **free**style **is** really **cool
*I **love** to swim **laps** up and **down** the **pool***
On the beats, alternately clap hands together and then against thighs

Swim! Swim!
Bend forward and "swim" with arms

*Swim-swim—**Turn**!*
Swim and then clap hands up high

Swim! Swim!
Bend forward and "swim" with arms

*Swim-swim—**Turn**!*
Swim and then clap hands up high

To end

***Ex**er**ci**sing is the **way** to **go**!*
*So **choose** your **sport** and*
On the beats, alternately clap hands together and then against thighs

***GO GO GO**!!*
Raise fists up high while chanting enthusiastically

VARIATIONS

- When the children are first learning this one, you could have them follow you. First chant part 1 of the verse, which the group then repeats. Then do the corresponding actions, which the group then imitates.

- Encourage students to write their own "Favorite Sport" chant—an engaging creative writing activity.

48

My Sweet Old Aunt

A cumulative movement game—with each new movement, you keep doing all the preceding ones. Sure to get you and your group laughing!

GRADE LEVEL

K–3

SKILLS PRACTICED

Focusing, listening, self-control, coordination

MATERIALS NEEDED

None

PREPARING STUDENTS FOR SUCCESS

- Practice saying the words and actions together.

- Practice staying in one place while moving your body gently.

- Each time you practice, try adding one more verse.

WORDS

You sing or chant each line, and the children echo it. A new motion accompanies each verse.

My sweet old aunt
Went to old Japan
And brought me back
This paper fan
Wave one hand back and forth in a fanning motion

My sweet old Aunt
Went to old Algiers
And brought me back
These pinking shears
Make cutting motion with two hands opening and closing

My sweet old aunt
Went to Holland, too
And brought me back
This wooden shoe
Stomp one foot

My sweet old aunt
Went to the county fair
And brought me back
This rocking chair
Rock body back and forth

My sweet old aunt
Went to Guadeloupe
And brought me back
This Hula-hoop
Pantomime hula hooping

My sweet old aunt
Went to Kalamazoo
And brought me back
Some gum to chew
Pantomime gum chewing

My sweet old aunt
Went to Timbuktu
And brought me back
*Some friends **like you**!!!*
Point to each other and laugh together!

VARIATIONS

- Invite children to create their own verses.

- Find the places you name on the map or globe.

My sweet old aunt___ went to old Ja - pan___ and brought me back___ this pa-per fan!

49 # My Two Hands

A transition activity that helps children settle down quickly. Great to use after an activity or energizer that may have them revved up.

GRADE LEVEL

K–3

SKILLS PRACTICED

Focusing, listening, self-control

MATERIALS NEEDED

None

PREPARING STUDENTS FOR SUCCESS

Practice saying the words and actions together.

WORDS

My two hands go clap clap clap
Clap with the words

My two feet go tap tap tap
Look down and point to feet and tap them on the ground

My two hands go thump thump thump
Thump hands on chest

My two feet go jump jump jump
Look down, point to feet, and jump up and down

My one body turns around
Hold one finger up and turn whole body around

And quietly sits down
Quietly sit down

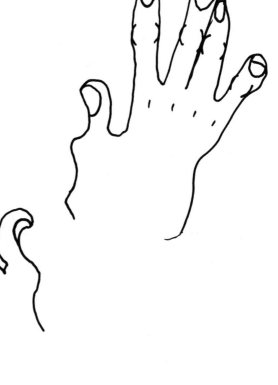

Never-Ending Word

Encourages team-work while children have fun and practice literacy skills.

GRADE LEVEL

3–6

SKILLS PRACTICED

Vocabulary, spelling, categorizing, creativity

MATERIALS NEEDED

Optional chart and markers to record student brainstorming

PREPARING STUDENTS FOR SUCCESS

- When beginning this activity, you might want to brainstorm words that belong to a theme and list them on a chart for students' reference.

- Discuss what will happen if two students pop up at the same time with the same (or a different) word.

- Talk about how to take care of each other when someone makes a mistake, cannot think of a word, or repeats a word (if you have chosen the "no repeats" challenge).

WORDS

The teacher begins by calling out a category and then chanting an item that fits into it. When a student has a word that fits into that category and that starts with the **last** letter of the previous word that was chanted, that child pops up and says the word.

For example:

Teacher: *Okay! It's time for our Never-Ending Word. Today's category is Fruits and Vegetables. Orange!*

Student 1 *Eggplant!*
Student 2 *Tomato!*
Student 3 *Onion!*

Etc.

Once students have popped up, they remain standing and can help others who have not yet thought of a word. The goals are for everyone to say at least one word that fits into the category and to end with the whole class standing.

VARIATIONS

- As the children chant, record each word on the board or chart paper, either in list format or as one long word.

- Incorporate some challenges:
  —No repeats
  —Children wait six seconds before chanting the next word
  —Children try to chant the next word before six seconds pass

"For young children, movement is a critical means of communication, expression, and learning. It is imperative that classroom teachers give children as many oppportunities as possible to be physically active and to learn through movement."

—Eloise Eliot, PhD, and Steve Sanders, PhD
PBS (Public Broadcasting System) teachers website

No-Talk Toss

This quick, silent game really helps students focus.

GRADE LEVEL

3–6

SKILLS PRACTICED

Self-control, focusing, coordination

MATERIALS NEEDED

A soft ball or bean bag

PREPARING STUDENTS FOR SUCCESS

- Discuss and practice safe ways to toss the ball to each other.

- Decide what will happen if someone misses the ball— how to respond helpfully but silently.

ACTIONS

1. Students stand at their desks. They must remain silent.

2. The leader tosses a small, soft ball to another student.

3. Students continue to pass the ball around the room randomly. Without talking or making any sound, students must find a way to communicate to the person to whom they want to throw the ball, so eye contact is essential.

4. If someone misses the ball, the catcher retrieves the dropped ball and continues on with the toss.

VARIATIONS

- Challenge students to toss the ball only to a classmate who has not had a turn and to remember who they tossed to and who tossed to them. Once all the students have had a chance to toss the ball, reverse that order.

- Set a time limit. Can we get through the whole class in less than a minute?

52   Now I'm Still

This creative movement can be done in a circle or with children spread about the room at desks or tables.

GRADE LEVEL

K–3

SKILLS PRACTICED

Rhythm, self-control, listening, creativity

MATERIALS NEEDED

Drum or other rhythm instrument

PREPARING STUDENTS FOR SUCCESS

- Practice saying the words together.

- Practice what it looks like to be "still."

- Model with a small group before having the whole group practice and participate.

- Model and practice actions that will keep students safe from bumping into each other.

- Share ways to maintain self-control while moving about the circle or classroom.

WORDS

Create a steady rhythm with a drum or other rhythm instrument as you chant the words. Students move to the beat slowly and then suddenly freeze in their position when you chant the word *still*. Once the children are reasonably still, continue chanting with another movement word, keeping the steady beat with your drum.

Adapt the beat of the drum to the children's energy level— for example, if they're overexcited, beat a slow, calming rhythm. You might choose to change the speed of the drum beat each time through, challenging the children to be ready to move to the new speed. Have fun with slow motion, too.

*Walk*ing, *walk*ing
Now I'm **walk**ing
*Walk*ing, *walk*ing
Now I'm still.

*Jump*ing, *jump*ing
Now I'm **jump**ing
*Jump*ing, *jump*ing
Now I'm still.

Continue with more movements!

To end
Slow the beat with each round, ending with several slow, calm beats.

Possible movements
Waving arms, bending forward with hands on hips, tip-toeing, clapping, side stepping, snapping fingers, twirling, jogging, skipping, hopping on one foot and then the other, sitting, blinking, yawning, whispering

VARIATIONS

- This energizer is fun to do outside with a large group. Establish boundaries and practice moving and staying within them. To encourage livelier movements and joyful noise in the fresh-air environment, use an instrument loud enough for the children to hear easily.

- Try it as a waiting-in-line activity.

Number Freeze

A great problem-solving activity that builds community.

GRADE LEVEL

3–6

SKILLS PRACTICED

Focusing, self-control, mathematics

MATERIALS NEEDED

None

PREPARING STUDENTS FOR SUCCESS

- Explain that the goal is to get the number of people standing to match the number the caller chooses. For example, if the caller chooses the number 8, the class tries to get 8 people standing.

- Have the students share their problem-solving strategies for success in this game, both before playing and after.

ACTIONS

Everyone begins sitting. A student calls out a number, anything smaller than the size of the class. Classmates try to get that number of people standing, while following these rules:

- No one may talk.

- Anyone may choose to stand at any time, but no one may stand for more than five seconds.

When the child who called out the number thinks the right number of classmates are standing, he calls out, "Everybody freeze!" He then counts the number of people standing to see if it matches the number he called out.

"Children need to move! Not just for the sake of their physical selves, but also for social, emotional and cognitive development."

—Rae Pica, children's physical activity specialist

Oh, My!

This engaging, rhythmic chant helps reinforce math concepts.

GRADE LEVEL

K–3

SKILLS PRACTICED

Focusing, listening, self-control, math, reading

MATERIALS NEEDED

Chart with words

WORDS AND ACTIONS

Students clap their thighs steadily to the beat throughout the chant, four claps per line.

Oh … my … ,
I want a piece of pie
The pie's too sweet
I want a piece of meat
Meat's too tough
I want to ride a bus
Bus is too full
I want to ride a bull
Bull might attack
I want my money back
Money's too green
I want a jelly bean
Jelly bean's too red
I want to go to bed
Bed's not made
I want some lemonade
Lemonade's too sour
Well, we've got the power to count to ten
And if we mess up we'll start all over again!

Now alternate between clapping hands and clapping thighs, chanting the numbers on the hand claps.

1, 2, 3, … 10!
Oh …
My!

- Substitute different numbers to count up to and create new rhymes for the two final lines.

- Modify for higher levels by incorporating skip-counting—for example:
  Well, we've got the power to count by fives
  and if we mess up we'll still be alive!
  5, 10, 15, etc.

- Have a helper point to each word on the chart.

- Divide the class in half and do as call and response.

- Invite the children to come up with their own rhymes.

55

Oliver Twist

With this one, the fun's in trying to keep up with the words and movements.

GRADE LEVEL

K–3

SKILLS PRACTICED

Focusing, listening, self-control

MATERIALS NEEDED

None

WORDS AND ACTIONS

Begin by chanting slowly together. Once the students know the words and motions, repeat again and again, each time getting faster and faster.

Oliver Twist, Twist, Twist
Put hands on hips and twist from side to side

Can't do this, this, this
Tap right foot and shake pointer finger of right hand

Touch his head, head, head
Touch head with hands

Touch his nose, nose, nose
Touch nose with hands

Touch his ears, ears, ears
Touch ears with hands

Touch his toes, toes, toes
Touch toes with hands

Opposite World Freeze Dance

A wordless creative movement energizer, helpful when an active group needs to let off steam.

GRADE LEVEL

K–6

SKILLS PRACTICED

Self-control, listening, balance, creativity

MATERIALS NEEDED

CD player

Lively music—instrumental or other

PREPARING STUDENTS FOR SUCCESS

■ Practice what it looks like to freeze. (Have younger children freeze with both feet on the floor.)

■ Model with a small group before having the whole group practice and participate.

■ Model and practice actions that will keep everyone from bumping into each other.

■ Share ways to maintain self-control while moving about the circle or classroom.

ACTIONS

When you turn the music on, the children do any movements or dance steps they choose. When you stop the music, the children freeze. If you "catch them" moving, they become part of Opposite World. This means they must freeze when the music plays, and when it stops, they can move as desired. Students may go back and forth between the two worlds as you continue to "catch them" moving when they shouldn't be.

VARIATION

Children remain seated and do the Hand Freeze Dance, the Elbow Freeze Dance, and any other "dances" that involve just one body part.

57 # Pass the Mask

A quiet yet delightful activity that incorporates drama and humor. Best done in a circle but also works well when waiting in a line. The benefit of the circle is that everyone in the group can watch and enjoy the many varieties of masks being put on and taken off.

GRADE LEVEL

K–6

SKILLS PRACTICED

Focusing, listening, self-control, dramatic expression, creativity

MATERIALS NEEDED

None

PREPARING STUDENTS FOR SUCCESS

Brainstorm various facial expressions that might accompany an emotion. List the kinds of emotions on a chart for reference during the game.

ACTIONS

The leader makes a face—for example, eyes and mouth wide open to show surprise—and then turns to the child next to him. The second child acknowledges the gesture by assuming the same expression. She then assumes a different expression and passes it to the next child in the circle, who imitates, chooses another to pass to the next child, and so on.

Continue around the circle until everyone has had a turn to put on a mask.

VARIATIONS

- Challenge the group to go all around the circle without repeating any masks.
- Simplify by passing the same mask all around the circle.

People to People

A rotating partner game that really gets you thinking and moving in creative ways!

GRADE LEVEL

3–6

SKILLS PRACTICED

Self-control, creativity, balance

MATERIALS NEEDED

None

PREPARING STUDENTS FOR SUCCESS

- Be sure to model and scaffold.

- The first few times you do this one with your students, it's best for you to be the caller.

- Practice these actions:
  —The people to people bridge
  —Changing partners safely
  —Safe body connections
  —"Extensions" for those body parts that are small or too close for comfort. Partners may connect parts using their thumb and pinky (with their middle three fingers folded down) as a connector, or extension.

WORDS AND ACTIONS

1. The group begins by standing and playfully clapping a steady beat together. Once everyone has the rhythm and tempo, the caller chants the chorus, with the group echoing each line:

   *The **name** of the **game**!*
   Group echoes

   *It's **always** the **same**!*
   Group echoes

   *It's **People** to **People**!!!*
   Group echoes

2. As the group echoes the words *People to People*, everyone moves to find a partner. Partners face each other and form a "bridge" by holding up their hands and placing their palms flat against their partner's palms.

3. The caller keeps clapping a steady beat. Once everyone has a partner, the caller begins calling out two body parts. Partners echo these words, while connecting their named body part with their partner's.

4. The caller then chants two new body parts to be connected, the group echoes, and the partners make those new body connections.

5. The chant continues, with the caller changing the two body parts with the beat three to five times, each time making the connections a little more challenging.

6. The caller chants *People to People!!*, the group echoes, and everyone moves to find a new partner.

7. Continue in this way for a few more rounds and then end with the following words:

*We've **fin**ished our **game**!*
Group echoes

*We **end** up the **same**!*
Group echoes

*With **People** to **People**!*
Group echoes

Possible body connections:

Beginner—connect same body parts

Shoulder to shoulder
Back to back
Elbow to elbow
Knees to knees

Intermediate—connect different body parts

Shoulder to back
Elbow to knee
Ankle to thumb
Hip to hand

Advanced—connect small or distant body parts, using "extensions" as desired

Nose to ear
Eyebrow to eyebrow
Ankle to hip
Cheek to chin

VARIATIONS

- Invite a student volunteer to be the caller and join in with your own "People to People" partner. Carefully discuss appropriate call-outs first!

- If the group is getting a little giggly and needs help refocusing, repeat the opening rhyme (*The name of the game, ...*) each time the children find new partners.

59 # Popcorn's in the Popper

You'll need some space for this one. Good for those rainy or wintery days when you're stuck inside and the children need to let out some energy.

GRADE LEVEL

K–3

SKILLS PRACTICED

Focusing, listening, self-control, patience

MATERIALS NEEDED

None

PREPARING STUDENTS FOR SUCCESS

- Best done in a circle but will work anywhere children have space to jump up and down safely.

- Talk about ways that popcorn has been made over the years: *In this song we're going to become popcorn, popping in a pot on top of a stove.*

- Teach the first part of the song and have one or two children model the three actions. Have more children practice in small groups of four to six. Build up to half the class jumping up and down together safely. Half the class can then be the popcorn chefs and say the chant, while the other half become the popcorn poppers and jump up and down when the song signals them to do so.

WORDS AND ACTIONS

Sort the children into two groups—chefs and poppers. Begin with poppers lying still on the floor, curled up like popcorn kernels (on backs with arms and legs drawn in tightly or just crouched down with arms drawn tightly around knees). Chefs can stand or sit anywhere.

Chefs: *First you pour in the oil*
Pantomime pouring oil into a pot

Poppers quietly echo: *Pour in the oil*

Chefs: *Sprinkle in the popcorn*
Pantomime sprinkling popcorn into pot

Poppers quietly echo: *Sprinkle in the popcorn*

Chefs: *Cover up the pan*
Pantomime covering the pan

Poppers quietly echo: *Cover up the pan*

Chefs: *Turn up the heat!*
Pantomime turning up the heat

Poppers quietly echo: *Turn up the heat!*

Chefs: Chant the rest of the song on their own while rubbing
their hands together as the poppers begin wiggling a bit:
Sizzle *Sizzle Sizzle Sizzle*
Sizzle *Sizzle Sizzle Sizzle*
Sizzle *Sizzle* **Sizzle Sizzle**

Chefs: **Pop**!!!
Do one loud clap

Poppers: Jump up and down like a piece of popcorn popping

Chefs continue chanting and clapping to

The popcorn's in the popper
Let it pop pop pop!

The popcorn's in the popper
Let it pop pop pop!

[Repeat]

Pop—pop—pop—pop!
Now
It's
Time to **stop***!*

Chefs: End the clapping with one last loud **clap** on the word "**stop**!"

Poppers: Stop jumping, curl up on the floor like pieces of popcorn, and lie still.
Can lie on back and draw arms and legs in or just crouch down with
arms drawn in against chests.

60 Pop-Up Number

Number fun
for all ages.

GRADE LEVEL

K–6

SKILLS PRACTICED

Focusing, listening, self-control, math

MATERIALS NEEDED

None

WORDS

Select a number from 1 through 10—say 4. Begin with everyone sitting, either in a circle or at their desks.

First child: *1*

Second child: *2*

Third child: *3*

Fourth child, popping up (jumping to a standing position): *4!*

Starting again at 1, the children still sitting continue counting around the room or circle, until all have popped up. Can anyone predict who'll be the last one sitting?

VARIATIONS

■ Child popping up calls out *Pop!* instead of the chosen number.

■ Do in reverse—begin standing and end up sitting. The child with the chosen number can call out "Melt!" and sink to a sitting position.

■ Adapt for older students by using prime numbers, multiples of 7, numbers divisible by 12, etc., as the number to pop on.

Rainstorm

It's amazing how much this noise-making activity sounds like the real thing!

GRADE LEVEL

K–6

SKILLS PRACTICED

Focusing, listening, self-control

MATERIALS NEEDED

None

WORDS AND ACTIONS

Begin by playfully engaging the children: *I am the Storm Master! As I do an action, you will copy me, and before you know it, we will have a rainstorm right here in our classroom!* Then start the actions. As you change each action and the sounds become louder, describe the rainstorm building in strength and then dying down; for example, *First comes the wind, then the soft rain. Next comes the hard rain, and then comes the thunder …*

As the storm builds:

Rub hands on thighs (light wind)
Rub hands together (stronger wind)
Snap fingers (soft rain)
Clap hands softly (hard rain)
Clap hands loudly (even harder rain—pouring now)
Slap thighs loudly (soft thunder)
Stomp feet (loud thunder)

Reverse sounds as the storm dies down:

Slap thighs loudly
Clap hands loudly
Clap hands softly
Snap fingers
Rub hands together
Rub hands on thighs

VARIATIONS

- Point to a new group for each action—you'll need seven groups. Each group continues its sound as the next group begins theirs.

- Invite a child to be the "Storm Master."

Ram Sam Sam

A nonsense song or chant to enjoy any time of day.

GRADE LEVEL

K–3

SKILLS PRACTICED

Focusing, listening, self-control

MATERIALS NEEDED

Optional: Chart with words

PREPARING STUDENTS FOR SUCCESS

- Practice saying the words and actions together slowly.
- As students show more success, try saying the words faster, louder, softer, slower, etc.

WORDS

A **Ram** Sam **Sam**
A **Ram** Sam **Sam**
Ghoolie **Ghoolie** Ghoolie **Ghoolie** Ghoolie
Ram Sam **Sam!**

A **Ram** Sam **Sam**
A **Ram** Sam **Sam**
Ghoolie **Ghoolie** Ghoolie **Ghoolie** Ghoolie
Ram Sam **Sam!**

A **Raffi!**
A **Raffi!**
Ghoolie **Ghoolie** Ghoolie **Ghoolie** Ghoolie
Ram Sam **Sam!**

A **Raffi!**
A **Raffi!**
Ghoolie **Ghoolie** Ghoolie **Ghoolie** Ghoolie
Ram Sam **Sam!**

ACTIONS—SITTING DOWN

Ram Sam Sam: Make two fists and gently tap them together, alternating which fist is on top when you chant the next line beginning with "Ram"

Ghoolie Ghoolie: Hold arms bent at elbows in front of you and roll forearms around one another

A Raffi: Lift arms high above you

ACTIONS—STANDING UP

Ram Sam Sam: Stomp your feet alternatively to the beat

Ghoolie Ghoolie: Twirl around

A Raffi: Jump up, look up, and reach your hands up high

VARIATIONS

■ Sit down or stand up, depending on your group's energy.

■ Sing as a round.

63 Robot Rap

A cumulative movement game—with each new movement, you keep doing all the preceding ones. Fun with a unit on inventions, or anytime you just want to be a little silly.

PREPARING STUDENTS FOR SUCCESS

- Practice saying the chant together in a clipped monotone.

- Talk about how robots move stiffly, and then model and practice actions for each verse.

- Practice freezing when *Robots at attention* is chanted.

- Share ways to maintain self-control and stay in one place while moving.

WORDS AND ACTIONS

What would you do if a robot came to tea?
Just look at me and a robot you will see!
Stand and chant or sing the words together

Robots at attention!
Stand straight

Robots let's begin!
Salute

Right arm!
Keep right arm against body, bend up and down at elbow

What would you do if a robot came to tea?
Just look at me and a robot you will see!
Chant or sing the words while right arm keeps moving

Robots at attention!
Drop right arm to side and stand straight

Robots let's begin!
Salute

Right arm, left arm!
Begin bending right elbow as before and add the same motion with left elbow

Continue repeating chant and add on one new movement pattern at a time as you do the following motions:

Right foot
Lift right leg up and then put it down

Left foot
Lift left leg up and then put it down

Head up! Head down!
Tip the head back to look up at the ceiling and then forward to look down at the floor

Turn around
Turn around once

***Sit down**!!*
Sit

VARIATIONS

- Extend to include other robot actions.

- Stiffly march around the room when saying *right foot, left foot* instead of staying in place. First model and practice safely moving around the classroom.

- Try being ragdolls instead of robots.

What would you do   if   a   ro-bot came to   tea?   Ro-bots at at-ten-tion!   Ro-bots, let's be-gin!
Just   look   at me, and a   ro-bot you will see!

Row Your Boat

Another old favorite with a surprising twist.

GRADE LEVEL

K–6

SKILLS PRACTICED

Focusing, listening, self-control, reading

MATERIALS NEEDED

Chart with words

PREPARING STUDENTS FOR SUCCESS

- Make sure everyone knows the words and tune.

- Gather and share ideas on friendly things to do or say if someone makes a mistake and says a word when they're not supposed to.

WORDS AND ACTIONS

Tell students that every time they sing the song, they'll drop one word from the end. Using a song chart, cover each word as you remove it from the verse.

Round 1

Row, row, row, your boat
Gently down the stream
Merrily, merrily, merrily, merrily
Life is but a dream!

Round 2

Row, row, row, your boat
Gently down the stream
Merrily, merrily, merrily, merrily
Life is but a …

Round 3

Row, row, row, your boat
Gently down the stream
Merrily, merrily, merrily, merrily
Life is but …

Continue the rounds, dropping one word with each round.

Last round

Row …

VARIATIONS

- Try another song, such as "White Coral Bells" or the first verse of "Farmer in the Dell."

- Instead of dropping a word each time, drop a whole line.

Save the Earth

Children like memorizing and moving to this thematic chant, especially in the spring when Earth Day is near.—*Original by the author*

GRADE LEVEL

K–3

SKILLS PRACTICED

Focusing, listening, self-control, reading

MATERIALS NEEDED

Chart with words

PREPARING STUDENTS FOR SUCCESS

Practice saying the words and doing the actions together.

WORDS AND ACTIONS

Begin with everyone standing, chanting together with vigor and volume as they clap their thighs for the beat.

*Super*man,
*Won*der Woman,
*Pow*er Rangers *too!*
We can be a *super*hero
Just like *you!*
We …
Can save …
The Earth!
Silent beat (thigh clap only; no words)

Yeah, we …
Can save …
The Earth!
Silent beat (thigh clap only; no words)

Do this last part twice through:

Leader calls, group echoes

Reduce!
Group echoes, raising right fist
Reuse!
Group echoes, raising left fist
Recycle!
Group echoes, clasping hands together over the tops of their heads

Set the Table

Children can have fun with this one when they're in line, in a circle, or at their desks.

SKILLS PRACTICED

Focusing, listening, self-control, rhythm, memory

MATERIALS NEEDED

Optional: Chart paper

PREPARING STUDENTS FOR SUCCESS

You may wish to list on a chart things you might put on a table when setting it for a meal. Students can then use this list for reference in case they feel stuck.

WORDS

Begin as a group, chanting and alternating thigh and hand claps:
Mabel, Mabel
Set the table
Just as fast
As you are able!

One at a time, children call out possible dinner table items. For example:
Plates!
Napkins!
Forks!
Knives!

Repeat the chant.

ACTIONS

1. Decide on a turn-taking order (around the circle to the right, up and down the rows from front to back, etc.).

2. Begin rhythmically clapping, alternating between clapping hands together and slapping hands against thighs.

3. Together, say the chant.

4. On the hand clap, the first person names an item that goes on the table.

5. Continue with three more people naming items on the hand clap.

6. Repeat the chant.

7. Now the next four people in order add things to the table that are different from what was already chanted.

8. Repeat from step 2, seeing if you can get through the whole class with no repeats and keeping with the beat. (It's harder than you think!)

"Along with physical education classes, students need physical activity opportunities throughout the school day."

—National Association for Sport and Physical Education

Shake It

This improv game releases energy and promotes originality.

GRADE LEVEL

3–6

SKILLS PRACTICED

Self-control, creativity

MATERIALS NEEDED

None

PREPARING STUDENTS FOR SUCCESS

- Brainstorm multiple ways the body can shake, even in just one part, such as the hand (up and down, side to side, fingers stretched out or in a fist), or one area, such as the hips (side to side, forward and back, around in circles, as if using a Hula-hoop).

- Practice a few body shakes with the class.

ACTIONS

Students begin standing, preferably in a circle. A leader begins by shaking one particular part of her body. For example, her foot may begin to shake fiercely. Then she uses eye contact to signal another player in the circle and "throws" the shake to that player. This person receives the shake in the same body part and then gradually moves the shake to another body part. For example, the shake might travel up the leg until it eventually reaches and rests in the hip. Once the shake is firmly established in this new body part, the student throws it to a new player, and the cycle continues.

The challenge is get through the whole class without repeating any shaking movements. If you do have repeats, encourage the students to come up with new ways to shake that part of the body.

End the energizer with all the students shaking their whole bodies. Everyone counts down from five and tries to be still when they get to zero.

Shake It Down

68

A great, rhythmic way to loosen up bodies. It also reinforces math concepts!

GRADE LEVEL

3–6

SKILLS PRACTICED

Counting, division, rhythm, self-control, balance

MATERIALS NEEDED

None

PREPARING STUDENTS FOR SUCCESS

Invite students to share ways to maintain balance and self-control while staying in one place.

WORDS AND ACTIONS

Chant and count with vigor!

1, 2, 3, 4, 5, … 16!
Stand and lift your right hand up high and shake it sixteen times
Repeat three times—with left hand, right foot, left foot

Cut!
Slice or cut right hand down on left palm

1, 2, 3, 4, 5, 6, 7, 8!

Lift your right hand up high and shake it eight times
Repeat three times—with left hand, right foot, left foot

Cut!
Slice or cut right hand down on left palm

1, 2, 3, 4!

Lift your right hand up high and shake it four times
Repeat three times—with left hand, right foot, left foot

Cut!
Slice or cut right hand down on left palm

1, 2!

Lift your right hand up high and shake it twice
Repeat three times—with left hand, right foot, left foot

Cut*!*
Slice or cut right hand down on left palm

1!
Lift your right hand up high and shake it once
Repeat three times—with left hand, right foot, left foot

Cut*!*
Slice or cut right hand down on left palm

Shake it down*!*
Shake whole body from top to bottom!

VARIATIONS

- Do in a circle formation, in an activity known as "Lean on Me." While shaking your right hand, place your left hand on the shoulder of the person to your left. Then switch, shaking your left hand while "leaning" on the person to your right.

- Here's a challenge: Think of compound words (for example, classroom, doorway, playground) or multisyllabic words (calculator, monopoly) that can be "cut" into smaller words or into syllables. Try chanting just these smaller words or syllables and shaking them down.

- Shake down your spelling words, letter by letter, in the same way. Have fun!

69 Shante Ohm

This chant uses yoga movements, but you can substitute any simple movements for those who don't know yoga.

PRONUNCIATION

Shante: **shŏn**-tē
Ohm: **ōm**

GRADE LEVEL

K–6

SKILLS PRACTICED

Focusing, listening, self-control, coordination, creativity

MATERIALS NEEDED

None

PREPARING STUDENTS FOR SUCCESS

Practice the simple movements or yoga poses you want to use.

WORDS

For each verse, the leader does a simple motion or yoga pose while chanting the words. Then everyone repeats the words together while doing the motion or pose.

POSSIBLE YOGA POSES

Crescent Moon, Eagle, Tree, Triangle, Warrior 1, Warrior 2

Here's the chant with some simple motions:

Shante Shante **Ohm**
*Shante **Ohm***
*Shante **Ohm***
Clap hands gently on thighs

Shante Shante **Ohm**
*Shante **Ohm***
*Shante **Ohm***
Move hands left and then right

Shante Shante **Ohm**
*Shante **Ohm***
*Shante **Ohm***
Take two steps left and two steps right

Shante *Shante* **Ohm**
Shante **Ohm**
Shante **Ohm**
Touch the floor and then reach for the sky

Continue with other simple moves or yoga poses. Close with one long "Ohm" while standing still with hands at sides.

VARIATIONS

- Students may take turns being the leader.

- On the last **ohm**, students can point to another student, who then becomes the leader.

Share the Light

A nice, calming activity to start the day or to end it at a closing circle.

GRADE LEVEL

K–6

SKILLS PRACTICED

Self-control, focusing, creativity

MATERIALS NEEDED

None

PREPARING STUDENTS FOR SUCCESS

- Talk with children about what "calm" and "relaxed" mean to them. (If necessary, help them understand the words first.) How do their bodies feel when they're calm? When do they feel most relaxed? Do they have a favorite place that helps them feel calm and relaxed? What do they do to calm themselves?

- Share ideas about imagining. What helps us construct vivid pictures in our minds?

- You may wish to begin this exercise by asking students to take a few deep breaths to help them relax.

WORDS

Students may be in a circle or spread about the room. Have them stand up comfortably, feet slightly apart, eyes closed. Then lead them through a guided imagery.

Make believe you have a small sun inside your head. Imagine this sun's light and energy slowly filling your head, then moving gently into your neck, then spreading into your chest, your shoulders . . . , your arms . . . , your hands . . . , your hips . . . , your legs . . . , your feet . . . , your toes. Imagine the warm and gentle light filling your whole body . . .

Now that the sun has filled your whole body, imagine its warmth and light shining out of you, through your eyes ... , through your fingers ... , through your toes ... , and this light begins to fill up the whole room. Now imagine the light filling up our whole school ... , the whole street ... , the whole neighborhood, the whole city ... , the whole state ... , the whole country ... , the whole world. Now imagine even more ... picture this warm light reaching up into the skies, up to the moon ... , beyond the sun ... , filling the whole universe.

Open your eyes ... let's continue to share the light!

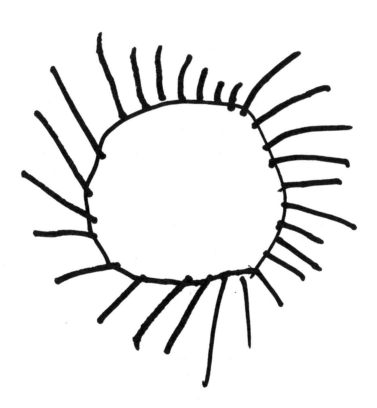

71 Shark Attack

Here's a pantomime activity that's pure fun anytime, but especially when the class is studying oceans.

GRADE LEVEL

3–6

SKILLS PRACTICED
Dramatic expression, humor, self-control

MATERIALS NEEDED

None

PREPARING STUDENTS FOR SUCCESS

- Talk about what "pantomime" means and practice the moves for the various beach characters.

- Discuss ways to practice self-control as you move through the story-song.

WORDS AND ACTIONS

Have the children stand, either at their desks or in a circle. For a more dramatic effect, exaggerate the first word in a slower beat. Once the "doo-doo"s start, pick up the pace.

As you chant the following opening verse, open and close pointer finger and thumb of either hand like a tiny shark's mouth. In subsequent verses, you'll replace the underlined words.

Opening verse

**Ba ... by shark**! _Doo-**doo**_
**Doo**-doo da **doo**
Baby **shark**! _Doo-**doo**_
**Doo**-doo da **doo**
Baby **shark**! _Doo-**doo**_
**Doo**-doo da **doo**
Baby **shark**!

Following verses

Repeat the opening verse with the same **Doo**-doo da **doo** rhythm, each time switching to the next word and action in the following list:

Mama: Hinge hands together at base of palms and open and close like a shark's mouth

Papa: Use same shark mouthing motion as for Mama, but make the "mouth" larger by lifting top hand up high

Surfer dude: Pantomime riding a wave—twist body side to side with arms out for balance

Saw a shark: With hand at forehead, pantomime looking far into the distance

Shark attack: With a frantic face, wave arms up and down

Swam away: Pantomime swimming back to shore

Where's my board?: Look around with bent elbows and hands up in the air

Surfin' shark: Pantomime riding a wave, but keep arms tight against body

Solar System Rap

This chant is especially fun when you're studying the planets.
—*Original by the author*

GRADE LEVEL

K–6

SKILLS PRACTICED

Focusing, listening, self-control, reading

MATERIALS NEEDED

Chart with words

Optional: Poster of the planets

PREPARING STUDENTS FOR SUCCESS

Practice saying the words and actions in small chunks before putting it all together.

WORDS

Refrain

Boom boom-ba **cha**-cha,
Boom boom-ba **cha**-cha,

Verse

Come **on** over **here** and **sit** right **down**
The **Solar Sys**tem's **coming** to **town**!

Chant refrain

We **start** with the **sun**
It's **really** a **star**
It's **mill**ions of **miles** away—that's **far**!

Chant refrain

Mercury, **Venus**, **Earth**, and **Mars**
Be**yond** the **pla**nets are **mill**ions of **stars**!
Mercury, **Venus**, **Earth**, and **Mars**
Milky Way, **planets**, **moons**, and **stars**

Chant refrain

And **don't** for**get**! The **big**gest pla**net**!
Jupiter! **Jup**iter! **Ju-pi-ter**!

Chant refrain

Then comes the **one** with the **great** big **ring**.
Saturn's the **one** that **makes** me **si-i-i-ng**!

Chant refrain

*We're **al**most **done**!*
***Three** more to **go**!*
***Uran**us,*
Nep**tune, **and
*Plu-**to**!*
*Oh **No**! Oh **Joy**!*
*Plu-**to's***
*a **plan**etoid!!!*

ACTIONS

Boom boom-ba: With *boom* and *boom-ba*, stretch arms out to the right and pound fists gently together

Cha-cha: With each *cha*, stretch arms out to the left with fingers spread wide apart

Do these rhythmic motions as you repeat the refrain. For the rest of the chant, simply keep a steady beat by clapping your hands against your thighs.

On the word *sing*, raise your voice up high and hold the note for a dramatic four beats.

73 Song of the Day

A simple yet very effective way to help students clear their minds and transition from work or activity time to the circle or to their desks or tables. Any song works—as long as it's just two to three minutes long!

GRADE LEVEL

K–6

SKILLS PRACTICED

Focusing, listening, self-control

MATERIALS NEEDED

CD player and CD

PREPARING STUDENTS FOR SUCCESS

- Discuss and practice, if necessary, how to finish up a task and move on to what's happening next.

- Play the song for the children and explain that it will be their signal to begin moving to the circle, desks, tables, etc. They need to be in place by the time the song is finished.

ACTIONS

Play the song. If necessary, remind the children what they should be doing while the song is playing.

VARIATION

Change the song daily or weekly—whatever works best for your students.

Spelling Stroll

You may see spelling
test scores go up
with this one!

GRADE LEVEL

3–6

**SKILLS
PRACTICED**

Focusing, listening,
self-control, spelling

**MATERIALS
NEEDED**

Spelling list

PREPARING STUDENTS FOR SUCCESS

Talk about what to do if two students reach a chair at the
same time.

ACTIONS

Children stand up at their desks. Using a spelling or sight
word, the teacher begins by stating the word the class will
"stroll" to. Together, the group spells out that word, moving
from desk to desk or about the room and taking one step for
each letter. At the last letter of the word, students and teacher
quickly and carefully sit down at the seat they're nearest to.
One person will be left standing. That person then becomes
the caller and chooses another word for the group to spell
together from the spelling list. The stroll continues until the
list has been completed.

VARIATIONS

Do with skip-counting and math facts. For example, the
teacher can call out "7 × 12!" The group then skip-counts
together by 12's seven times, taking one step for each number (12, 24, 36, 48, etc.).

Sports on the Move

Lively fun, especially on days when the children don't have P.E. or can't go outside.

GRADE LEVEL

K–6

SKILLS PRACTICED

Self-control, balance, coordination

MATERIALS NEEDED

None

PREPARING STUDENTS FOR SUCCESS

- For younger children, talk about what "imitate" means.
- Model and practice different sports moves.
- Practice having the children imitate a leader.
- Emphasize moving in ways that are safe for indoor play.

WORDS AND ACTIONS

Call out a sport and begin making movements that go with that sport as students imitate you. Give each sport about 30 seconds.

EXAMPLES

Basketball: Dribble with fingertips, dribble through legs, dribble around back, make a jump shot and follow through, make a bounce pass, make a chest pass, make an overhead pass, do a defensive slide to front

Soccer: Shoot on goal (practice with both feet), pass with inside of foot, pass with outside of foot, do long banana kick, juggle imaginary soccer ball, trap ball with thigh, trap ball with feet

Baseball or softball: Swing a bat, wind up and pitch, field a ground ball, catch a fly ball, play imaginary catch

Tennis: Hit with forehand, hit with backhand, serve, volley

Volleyball: Serve, set, dig, spike

Football: Make quarterback long pass, make short pass, catch imaginary ball, kick field goal, punt, catch a punt, block

Other sports possibilities: Golf, racecar driving, lacrosse

VARIATION

Invite the students to teach the class their sports moves.

Switch!

A fun and purposeful thumb-and-pointer-finger drill that helps integrate brain hemispheres. Harder than you think!

GRADE LEVEL

3–6

SKILLS PRACTICED

Self-control, coordination, focusing

MATERIALS NEEDED

None

PREPARING STUDENTS FOR SUCCESS

The directions are simple and straightforward, but mastering this energizer takes some practice. Some learners will accomplish this quickly; others will take more time, or perhaps feel as if they'll never get it. Discuss what kind, encouraging words we can give to each other as we learn.

ACTIONS

1. The children place their right hand out in front of them, with the thumb up and all the fingers curled in. They place their left hand out in front of them, with their pointer finger out and the thumb and other fingers curled in.

2. Once all the children are ready, call out "Switch!"

3. Instantly, everyone switches the pointer fingers and thumbs of their hands so that the right hand now has the index finger pointing and the left hand has the thumb up.

4. On the next "Switch!" the right hand will have the thumb up and the left will have the pointer finger out.

5. Continue in this way, with children changing between finger and thumb on both hands each time you call out "Switch!"

VARIATIONS

- Pair students up and have them take turns saying *Switch*.

- Invite the students to come up with other hand or body parts to play the game with.

Tarzan

A silly chant that'll get your students moving and giggling.

GRADE LEVEL

K–3

SKILLS PRACTICED

Self-control, creativity, reading

MATERIALS NEEDED

Chart with words

PREPARING STUDENTS FOR SUCCESS

- Talk about ways to maintain self-control during the chant.

- Agree on what actions are appropriate for your classroom.

WORDS

Choose a leader to call out each line, which the group repeats.

Tar … zan!
Swingin' on a rubber band
Tar … zan!
Fell into a frying pan
Now Tarzan has a tan!
Ja … ane!
Flying in an air-o-plane
Ja … ane!
Crashed into a highway lane
Now Jane has a pain!
And Tarzan has a tan!
Chee … tah!
Rockin' to the beat-a
Chee … tah!
Got bit by an amoeba
Now Cheetah is Velveeta!
And Jane has a pain!
And Tarzan has a tan!
And my story's at its end!

ACTIONS

Children stand while chanting and may pantomime each line as desired.

VARIATION

Once the class knows the chant well, divide the group in half. The first group can be the leaders and the second can be the "echoers."

Tar - zan!__ Swing-in' on a rub - ber band! Tar - zan!__

Fell in - to a fry - in' pan! Now Tar - zan has a tan!

78 Terry the Towel

A silent, calming, "follow the leader" activity that incorporates humor, creativity, and relaxation. Great for a needed break in between reading or writing activities, or before or after quiet time.

GRADE LEVEL

K–3

SKILLS PRACTICED

Focusing, observation

MATERIALS NEEDED

A soft towel about the size of a kitchen towel. Tie a simple knot at the top of the towel, creating what looks like a puppet's head. Make sure there's a good amount of fabric left below the knot.

PREPARING STUDENTS FOR SUCCESS

Talk about how important it is for our brains and bodies to have a quiet, calming activity sometimes.

WORDS AND ACTIONS

Hold up your towel puppet to the class. Begin with an introduction that may sound something like this: *I'd like to introduce you to my friend, Terry the Towel. Terry is here today to help us stretch and relax our hard-working muscles, bodies, and brains. I guarantee you'll feel great after joining Terry in some simple movements. All you have to do is follow Terry and do what she does. So let's begin!*

Have Terry look around the room as if greeting her guests. Begin with some simple movements with Terry—move her head slowly from side to side, up and down. Students then quietly follow with their own bodies the movements you make with Terry.

If the children have trouble understanding what Terry is doing, cue them with words (*Terry lifts her arm*) or by doing the movement yourself as you're making Terry do it.

OTHER POSSIBLE MOVEMENTS

Lift one side of the towel up slowly, then the other side. Students will raise and lower their arms at the same time.

With your other hand, form a "seat" for Terry. Now let Terry slowly stand up and down, bending and unbending her knees.

Have Terry jump up and down slowly.

Have fun with this! How many ways can you make Terry move?

VARIATIONS

Use different objects to make Terry's relatives: Kendra the Kerchief, Timmy the Tissue, Scarlet the Scarf

79

Tony Chestnut

A silly song with many variations in words and tune. Older children (third grade and up) may enjoy teaching it to younger ones.

GRADE LEVEL

K–3

SKILLS PRACTICED

Focusing, listening, self-control, homonyms

MATERIALS NEEDED

None

PREPARING STUDENTS FOR SUCCESS

Have some discussions on how words can sound the same but have different meanings. If appropriate for your students, you could introduce the concept of homonyms.

Sing the song together before adding the motions.

Important: Children younger than seven do not typically understand plays on words, so be prepared to explain the double meaning of the words in this song.

WORDS (Sung to the tune of Frère Jacques)

Tony Chestnut
Tony Chestnut
Tony knows
Tony knows
Tony knows I love you
Tony knows I love you
Tony knows
Tony knows

ACTIONS

Place hands on the parts of your body that are spoken in each word or syllable:

To ...	hands on toes
... ny	hands on knees
Chest	hands on chest
nut	hands on head
knows	hands on nose
I	hands point to eyes
love	hands cross over heart
you	point to a friend

Top It

This energizer promotes creative responses and playfulness with language.

GRADE LEVEL

3–6

SKILLS PRACTICED

Focusing, memory, language arts, creativity

MATERIALS NEEDED

None

PREPARING STUDENTS FOR SUCCESS

- Talk with the children about the concept of playful one-upmanship.
- Brainstorm possible topics.

WORDS

Begin by providing a topic that others will try to "top." You may also want to provide the first statement that others will try to top. For example, you might say *running* and then *I ran a mile this weekend....* In an around-the-room fashion, each student tries to "top" one or two parts of the previous statement. Fibbing is highly encouraged! For example:

Teacher: *It's time to top it! Our top it topic is running ...*

Student 1: *I ran a mile this weekend in 7½ minutes.*

Student 2: *I ran to school in 14 minutes.*

Student 3: *I ran 3 miles to school in 14 minutes.*

Student 4: *I ran 3 miles to school in 20 minutes in the pouring rain with no shoes on.*

Continue until all the children have had a turn.

VARIATIONS

- Connect to grammar: Will you change the subject? The adverb? The adjective?
- Record the sentences. The next day, have the students circle the changed words and identify their part of speech.

81 Walkie-Talkies

Great for a short stretch and break. Also a good way to give children a chance to catch up with each other after a vacation.

GRADE LEVEL

3–6

SKILLS PRACTICED

Cooperation, assertion, self-control

MATERIALS NEEDED

Chime or other auditory signal

PREPARING STUDENTS FOR SUCCESS

- Brainstorm conversational topics that are appropriate for school—for example, books you're reading, plans for the weekend, your proudest work so far this year.

- Practice how to safely move about the room to find a partner.

- Practice how to end a conversation: When you ring the chime the first time, students can say, for example, "Oh, there's the first chime; can we finish this conversation at recess?" or "I wish we had more time—let's talk at lunch." At the second chime, students begin quietly walking to their chairs. At the third chime, they're in their seats.

WORDS

Teacher: *It's Walkie-Talkie Time! Find a partner, start talking together, and then start heading back to your seats when you hear the first chime. By the third chime, you'll be in your seats.*

Children walk about the classroom and chat with each other using a topic from the list they generated. They can choose partners freely, or you can call out attributes for choosing partners; for example, choose a partner who has the same eye color, hair color, number of buttons, type of shoes, birthday month, number of letters in first name, etc.

VARIATION

Choose a conversational topic connected to the children's current studies.

The Wave

A lively energizer to build class creativity and cohesion. It's like the wave fans create at sporting events.

SKILLS PRACTICED

Rhythm, self-control, sequencing

MATERIALS NEEDED

None

PREPARING STUDENTS FOR SUCCESS

- Brainstorm, model, and practice appropriate actions that are respectful and manageable for all to do.

- Discuss and model starting the action when the person before you is halfway through.

- Share ways to maintain self-control while staying in one place and waiting for your turn.

ACTIONS

All students stand in a circle, with enough space between them to enable them to safely make the motions. (This can be a rough circle, with children standing around the perimeter of the classroom.) The leader models a movement, such as raising and then lowering the arms or clapping the hands gently together. One at a time, the students then repeat the movement.

Once the movement returns to the person who started it, the next person begins a new movement, which proceeds around the circle in the same way as the first movement. Continue in this way until several students have had an opportunity to come up with and perform a movement.

VARIATION

Have the children form two circles, one inside the other, with two leaders and the wave going through both circles simultaneously or jumping from one circle to another.

83 We're All Back Together Again

A welcoming song that can start your day off right.

GRADE LEVEL

K–3

SKILLS PRACTICED

Cooperation, language arts, listening

MATERIALS NEEDED

Chart with words

PREPARING STUDENTS FOR SUCCESS

To help children learn the words, you may decide to teach the second part first and then sing the whole song through together.

WORDS

1. Group echoes as leader sings each line

    Good morning!
    How are you?
    I'm so glad
    To see you!
    Let's sing and
    Be happy
    'Cause we're all back together again!

2. Everyone chants together

    With a one and a two
    Hold up one finger and then two

    And a how do you do?
    Pantomime a handshake

    With a big hello
    Give a big wave

    We're ready to go
    Push fist up in the air with excitement

    We're all back together again!
    Circle hand up and around, pointing to the group

VARIATIONS

- You can simply chant this song. Just change the word *sing* to *learn*.

- For the first part, divide the class in half and have one half lead while the other half echoes.

- Have the adults sing to the students.

- Have students join with a partner and do the motions together.

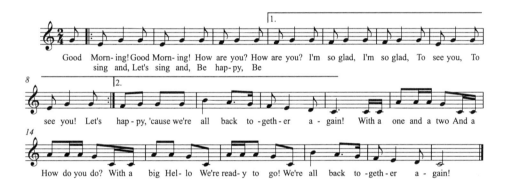

What's the Connection?

Here's a way to play with metaphorical language.

GRADE LEVEL

3–6

SKILLS PRACTICED

Listening, creativity, language arts

MATERIALS NEEDED

None

WORDS AND ACTIONS

Hold up an object and ask what the object has to do with one of your units of study. Students generate ideas about how the object might be related to the unit of study you've named. Answers may be serious or silly. For example:

Teacher: *What does this toothbrush have to do with math? What's the connection?*

Student 1: *We brush up on our math skills.*

Student 2: *Sometimes we have to brush away wrong answers.*

Student 3: *Math keeps our minds shiny.*

You can then ask another question using the same item, or ask a question using a new item.

VARIATIONS

- To boost the energy, students may stand up as they answer the question.

- If students find this difficult at first, partner them up or put them in small groups of three or four to brainstorm connections.

Which Direction?

Use this one to give your students practice with global directions, as well as to energize their bodies and brains.

GRADE LEVEL

3–6

SKILLS PRACTICED

Decision-making, global directions, self-control

MATERIALS NEEDED

For younger students: Primary directions (north, south, east, and west) written on chart paper

PREPARING STUDENTS FOR SUCCESS

- Review the directions and make sure all the children know which way to turn for each direction.

- For younger children, post each direction on the appropriate classroom wall.

- Talk about what children can do if they're unsure which way to turn.

WORDS AND ACTIONS

Begin standing. Call out a clue or question to which the answer is one of the directions—north, south, east, or west. Students quickly turn to face the correct direction. Begin with simple directions, such as:

Everybody, face north!
… south!
… east!
… west!

Then make the directions more challenging:
Face the direction the sun rises in …
Face the direction that Mrs. Jones's classroom is in …
The playground is to the …
The principal's office is to the …
Our town hall is to the …

VARIATIONS

- Incorporate exercise:
  Face north and do five jumping jacks
  Stretch to the west

- When students are comfortable with basic directions, add more complex ones: northwest, northeast, etc.

World Ocean Doo-Wop

The song and movements are fun anytime, but especially during a unit on oceans.
—*Original by the author*

GRADE LEVEL

K–6

SKILLS PRACTICED

Cooperation, language arts, self-control

MATERIALS NEEDED

Song chart

PREPARING STUDENTS FOR SUCCESS

- Introduce the song on the song chart.

- As with any detailed song with rich vocabulary, spend time discussing new terms before teaching the tune and movements.

- Sing the ocean names, one at a time, arpeggio style, and have the children echo you.

- Show them the "doo-wop-a-doo" movement and have them practice it: Put your palms together at your side and then point and sweep them downward and upward in front of you, like an ocean wave.

- Point to the words as you sing them, and as the children learn the repetitive tune, have them read it and sing it with you, incorporating the doo-wop movements where noted.

WORDS AND ACTIONS

Chorus

The leader sings the ocean names arpeggio style (each name at a slightly higher pitch than the last) and the group echoes.

Atlantic
Group echoes

Pacific
Group echoes

Indian
Group echoes

Arctic
Group echoes

Doo-wop-a-doo!
Group does the ocean wave movement

Verses

The world's oceans one by one—Doo-wop-a-doo!
Salt water, waves, sand, and sun—Doo-wop-a-doo!
The ocean beach is so much fun!—Doo-wop-a-doo!

Repeat chorus

Fish and whales and sharks do swim—Doo-wop-a-doo!
Coral reefs and exoskeletons—Doo-wop-a-doo!
It's an underwater jungle-gym!—Doo-wop-a-doo!

Repeat chorus

So much life in the great wide sea—Doo-wop-a-doo!
It's up to us to keep it clean and free—Doo-wop-a-doo!
Let's take part in our ecology!—Doo-wop-a-doo!

Repeat chorus

End with one last joyful *Doo-wop-a-doo!!!!*

VARIATION

Divide the class up into four groups. Assign an ocean to each group. When they sing their ocean, have them hold the note until all four oceans have been sung for a beautiful harmonious sound.

87 Worldwide Seven Continents

A fun way to teach or review the continents while taking a quick break.
—*Original by the author*

GRADE LEVEL

K–3

SKILLS PRACTICED

Focusing, listening, self-control, geography

MATERIALS NEEDED

World wall map or globe

PREPARING STUDENTS FOR SUCCESS

Practice identifing the seven continents on a map or globe.

WORDS

Hey all you expert ge**ographers**!
We're **gon**na take a **trip**
A**round** the **world**!
If **any**one **asks** you **where** we **went**,
Tell them the seven **con-ti-nents**!

North–America! (Groups echoes each continent
   as leader points to it on map or globe)
South–America!
Eur–ope!
As–ia!
Aus**tra**–lia!
Af-ri-ca!
I said **Af-ri-ca!**
Ant-**arc**-ti-ca!

That's what they **are!**
That's where we **went!**
The **worldwide** seven **con-ti-nents**!

Za Ziggy

A fun "follow the leader" game with a twist. Can you keep up with—but not get ahead of—the leader?

GRADE LEVEL

3–6

SKILLS PRACTICED

Focusing, listening, self-control, memorization, creativity

MATERIALS NEEDED

None

WORDS

Za *Ziggy*
Za *Ziggy*
Za *Po* **Po**

Za *Ziggy*
Za *Ziggy*
Za *Po* **Po**

Repeat as many times as desired.

ACTIONS

After the first time through the chant, the leader chooses a motion to demonstrate on the words *Po Po*. On the next repeat, the group imitates that motion, while the leader demonstrates a new *Po Po* motion. With each repeat from here on, the leader and the group are always doing different *Po Po* motions, with the group one *Po Po* motion behind the leader.

Za: Clap thighs
Ziggy: Clap hands
Po Po: Leader chooses a body motion

Some possible motions for "Po Po":

Round 1—Rolling arms
Leader and group all roll arms

Round 2—Waving arms above head
Leader waves arms, group rolls arms

Za Ziggy, cont.

Round 3—Moving arms from left to right
Leader moves arms from left to right, group waves arms above heads

Round 4—Snapping fingers
Leader snaps fingers, group moves arms from left to right

Round 5—Nodding head from left to right
Leader nods, group snaps fingers

Round 6—Bobbing head up and down
Leader bobs head, group nods heads left to right

Next-to-last round—Rolling arms (repeat of first round)
Leader rolls arms, group bobs heads

To end

Hold arms up in air straight in front of you
Leader folds arms, group rolls arms

Final round

Leader is quiet and stays still with arms folded
Group chants and ends with arms folded

RELATED RESOURCES

From Center for Responsive Schools, Inc.

Visit www.responsiveclassroom.org for details on these and other *Responsive Classroom* resources.

The Morning Meeting Book, 3rd edition, by Roxann Kriete and Carol Davis. 2014.

80 Morning Meeting Ideas for Grades K–2 by Susan Lattanzi Roser. 2012.

80 Morning Meeting Ideas for Grades 3–6 by Carol Davis. 2012.

99 Activities and Greetings: Great for Morning Meeting . . . and Other Meetings, Too! by Melissa Correa-Connolly. 2004.

Closing Circles: 50 Activities for Ending the Day in a Positive Way by Dana Januszka and Kristen Vincent. 2012.

Doing Math in Morning Meeting: 150 Quick Activities That Connect to Your Curriculum by Andy Dousis and Margaret Berry Wilson. 2010.

Doing Science in Morning Meeting: 150 Quick Activities That Connect to Your Curriculum by Lara Webb and Margaret Berry Wilson. 2013.

Doing Language Arts in Morning Meeting: 150 Quick Activities That Connect to Your Curriculum by Jodie Luongo, Joan Riordan, and Kate Umstatter. 2015.

Doing Social Studies in Morning Meeting: 150 Quick Activities That Connect to Your Curriculum by Leah Carson and Jane Cofie. 2017.

ABOUT THE AUTHOR

Susan Lattanzi Roser has been an educator since 1983. She taught pre-K through third grade for fifteen years, including in university lab school and magnet school settings. At the college level, Susan has taught courses in early childhood education as well as music and movement for young children. In 1998, Susan became a consulting teacher for Center for Responsive Schools (formerly Northeast Foundation for Children), teaching principals, teachers, and parents around the country about the *Responsive Classroom*® approach.

Susan received her BS in human development, counseling, and family studies from the University of Rhode Island and her MA in education from Lesley College, with a concentration in using the creative arts in teaching. The daughter of an artist and a physician/musician, Susan has been "energizing" all her life, finding ways to enhance learning for children and adults by weaving movement and the arts into her teaching.

With her husband Mark and her two boys, Will and Wes, Susan lives in Connecticut, where the family spends time together being creative in numerous ways, including painting, playing piano, bird watching, frog catching, dog sledding, hosting exchange students, and living life to its fullest.

ABOUT THE PUBLISHER

Center for Responsive Schools, Inc., a not-for-profit educational organization, is the developer of *Responsive Classroom*®, an evidence-based education approach associated with greater teacher effectiveness, higher student achievement, and improved school climate. *Responsive Classroom* practices help educators build competencies in four interrelated domains: engaging academics, positive community, effective management, and developmentally responsive teaching. We offer the following resources for educators:

Professional Development Services

- Workshops for K–8 educators (locations around the country and internationally)
- On-site consulting services to support implementation
- Resources for site-based study
- Annual conferences for K–8 educators

Publications and Resources

- Books on a wide variety of *Responsive Classroom* topics
- Free monthly newsletter
- Extensive library of free articles on our website

For details, contact:

Center for Responsive Schools, Inc.
85 Avenue A, P.O. Box 718
Turners Falls, Massachusetts 01376-0718

800-360-6332   www.responsiveclassroom.org
info@responsiveclassroom.org